THE MEDITERRANEAN SHORE

To Lawrence Durrell, kindred restless spirit, in admiration. **PH**

THE MEDITERRANEAN SHORE

Travels in Lawrence Durrell Country
Paul Hogarth

Introduction and Commentary by Lawrence Durrell

PAVILION
MICHAEL JOSEPH

FIRST PUBLISHED IN GREAT BRITAIN IN 1988 BY
PAVILION BOOKS LIMITED
196 SHAFTESBURY AVENUE
LONDON WC2H 8JL
IN ASSOCIATION WITH MICHAEL JOSEPH LIMITED
27 WRIGHTS LANE, KENSINGTON, LONDON W8 5TZ

DESIGNED BY DAVID DRIVER

BRITISH LIBRARY CATALOGUING IN PUBLICATION DATA
HOGARTH, PAUL
MEDITERRANEAN SHORE.
1. DURRELL, LAWRENCE – HOMES AND HAUNTS
2. VOYAGES AND TRAVELS
I. TITLE II. DURRELL, LAWRENCE
910 PR60007.U76Z/
ISBN 1–85145–200–1

PRINTED AND BOUND IN SPAIN BY CAYFOSA, BARCELONA

CONTENTS

'The grand object of travelling is to see the shores
of the Mediterranean' **Dr Samuel Johnson**

The chosen few who have been deeply involved in the various phases of
research and preparation of this book are especially deserving of my gratitude.
Among these should be counted Diana Robson-Smith whose unfailing
good humour and encouragement enabled me to survive many trials and
tribulations; Robin Rook whose lucid introductions to Lawrence Durrell's *oeuvre*
as well as his commentary – derived from conversations over several
days between the maestro and himself – add a further dimension to the book;
David Driver, who designed every aspect of its handsome appearance,
and last but certainly not least, Pavilion's editors, Susan Mitchell
and Maria Leach who kept a watchful eye on its progress.
Special thanks are due to Piers Rodgers, Secretary of the Royal Academy
of Arts, London; to Dr Victoria Solomidis, Cultural Attaché, Greek Embassy,
London; Mr Dmitris P. Tsitouras, Athens and Dr Youness El-Batrick,
Cultural Counsellor, Egyptian Embassy, London, for their help in facilitating
advice and hospitality. Others whose contributions were hardly less
invaluable are: Ms Maria Aspiotti, Corfu (*Prospero's Cell*); Ms Christina
Thayou of the Greek National Tourist Organization, Hania, Crete
(*The Dark Labyrinth*); John Hope and Penelope Hope-Durrell, Lindos
(*Reflections on a Marine Venus*); Mr and Mrs James W. Adams,
British Ambassador to Egypt, Mrs Sue Lyon of the Embassy staff,
Anthony Madeley, British Consulate, Alexandria; Mr Hazem Abu Sheleib,
General Manager, Regional Authority for Tourism Promotion, Alexandria,
Ms Aida Hassan of his staff; Mr Ashraf Jacob, St Marks & All Saints
Church of Alexandria; Emilio Ambron, Florence, Italy; Mr Hamdi Abdel
Ghaffar, Manager, Palestine Hotel, Montazah, Alexandria; Dr Mustapha Adly,
Royal Yacht Club of Egypt, Alexandria (THE ALEXANDRIA QUARTET);
Ms Maureen Ashley, London and Signor Marco De Bartholi, Marsala;
Ms Daphne Phelpps and Ms Antonietta Falanga, Taormina, Sicily
(*Sicilian Carousel*); Ms Fufi Trigata, St George Lycabettus Hotel, Athens (*Tunc*).
My thanks are also due to Ms Senga Shearer of Twicker's World,
who grappled with complicated and frequently changing travel arrangements
with commendable stoicism. **Paul Hogarth**

A WORD FROM THE ARTIST

Yet another year of my life has been spent depicting the life and landscape of distant lands. My previous travels for GRAHAM GREENE COUNTRY took me over oceans and jungles of four continents. This time, it has been a more exuberant, if more modest odyssey around the shores of the Mediterranean to depict the settings and locations of Lawrence Durrell's novels and travel-books.

Graham Greene and Lawrence Durrell, despite their differences as writers, have much in common. Both are storytellers with a scrupulous concern for what Durrell has defined as the spirit of place. This involves a more than appreciative eye for idiosyncratic towns and cities, for unusual buildings and above all, for the oddities of human character: all very much to my taste but not without their problems. Memory can play tricks on a writer, especially if he has, like Lawrence Durrell, written about places years after he has lived in them. For although we conferred to identify what was 'from the stockpot' and what actually existed, he urged me to use my imagination whenever necessary. Occasionally, I was compelled to do so, sometimes only to find that a certain building really did exist after all, but in another place.

There was also the problem of portraying a way of life long since dissolved in the mists of time. I had hoped to capture something of the nostalgic romanticism of THE ALEXANDRIA QUARTET. Those superb novels introduced me, as they did most readers, unforgettably to that private world of the late Thirties and early Forties. That almost all their settings and locations might no longer exist simply did not occur to me. But then I should have realized how brutally irrevocable social change can be. I might as well have attempted to recreate the world of Dostoevsky. Like Dostoevsky's St Petersburg, Lawrence Durrell's Alexandria has long since gone. The only difference is that much of the old Russian capital remains to be seen; relatively little remains of mid-twentieth-century Alexandria.

Fortunately, more than enough remained elsewhere. And once again, it was fascinating to discover that so much still existed, more or less unchanged. Lawrence Durrell has, of course, had the advantage. In country after country, on island after island, this great writer has savoured the language, the landscape and the turbulent history of the Mediterranean. Whilst I, the peripatetic observer that I essentially am, have had to content myself by creating images that reflect but fragments of his much-lived life. Whenever I could, I made full use of the occasional opportunity to inject them, or should I say, imbue them with my own deep love for the Mediterranean Shore.

Paul Hogarth

INTRODUCTION

'Painting persuades by thrilling the mind and the optic nerve simultaneously, whereas words connote, mean something however approximate and are influenced by their associative value. The spell they cast intends to master things – it lacks innocence. They are the instruments of Merlin or Faust. Painting is devoid of this kind of treachery – it is an innocent celebration of things, only seeking to inspirit and not coerce.' (Livia).

When I was told one day that an unusually imaginative publisher had mooted my name in connection with a book about the Mediterranean shore which would involve the work of Paul Hogarth, I allowed my heart to do a double somersault of surprised elation. I knew his work – that blithe and tender line backed up with seraphic colouring. It seemed too good to be true. Would he accept? And if he did, would my own work do full justice to that of one of the greatest contemporary masters of water-colour? Hum. But the idea was exciting; it seemed to me that I could already hear his exclamations of surprise and delight – for everything in the Mediterraean and Greece in particular is slightly better than anything in nature has a right to be. How to deal with it truthfully? You are on the razor's edge. The slightest trace of conscious overplaying, of showing off, would bring you to that fatal conjunction where the proverbial slips twixt cup and lip take place.

Would he accept a task so full of hazards? Perhaps the very dangers would constitute a challenge and persuade him to? (They have!) I knew that if his surprising talent were let loose in Greece he would come out of the venture with his pockets full of rainbows. What a compliment, too, for a writer whose whole working life has been lived in the shadow of the Parthenon, so to speak, to have his own private collection of Hogarths – all those magnetic places like monograms of ancient happiness retouched by the brush of memory, stirred into new life. I felt sure he would coax wonders of charm and insight from this much treated subject. He is, as a painter, particularly appropriate to his subject for he is something more than an illustrator. These large and fluent *aquarelles* are full of insight – they are touched by the divining rod, and it is extraordinary that such speed of execution is matched by so much insight and intuition, for the whole volume of the work constitutes a fabulous commentary on modern Greece in all its defenceless loveliness.

It is a demon of a subject and he has done it full justice with precision and tenderness. As a painter he has always had a weakness for the spontaneous touch, and many of these beauties come from their unexpectedness – unexpected as a dimple, say, on the cheek of an island child! So original in their freshness; newly minted by that prolific, scintillating talent!

It was not proposed to try and master-mind the *cher maître*, to persecute him with too much donnishness; but we would try to work along the lines of an agreed itinerary which allowed flexibility of approach – for the islands are many and various as to history. But meet we must and did.

And have! He so much resembled Henry Miller at forty that we could hardly fail to get on. Moreover, I found that he had never treated his subject in depth as yet and was looking forward to the experience with the right mixture of irreverent joy – he welcomed the obvious dangers of sloppiness and sentiment with fearless self-confidence. He gave the right impression of an artist who had heard the cocks of Attica from the Acropolis already. I read through the proposed itinerary of his trip with lustful envy. Whatever happened to my side of the venture, I was confident now that he could carry the whole weight of our book on his own back! This confidence set me free to dream up old memories of the past, for there was always the question of depth of historical focus – after all, each one of us selects his own epicentre from which to judge a person or a place. My association with Greece was more than fifty years old. My memory was a huge lumber-room full of unclassified and undocumented happenings – wherever the artist touched with his brush there would be a bruised place, an old freakish memory, a forgotten melody . . . I only felt reassured that things would match up when I received Hogarth's first postcards from Greece itself – for after a few meetings, his conviction that we must get moving drove him to go off like a rocket, to dive like a swimmer into the world of Greece. I knew now that the level of his discourse would capture the truth – so great was its exuberance. And now I was beginning to enjoy Greece through his eyes. 'It's impossible to describe – it must be seen to be believed – and excused, if possible!' He was on that fabulous giant's causeway, the sky-staircase of Santorini – the huge crater of an extinct volcano. He was discovering that here the sea and the sky meet as nowhere else. Here I was once able to offer the quiet poet Seferis* a drink, in exchange for which he read me his great poem about Santorini aloud while the almond-blossom sifted down into our plates and from a nearby tavern came the scribbling and scratching of *bouzouki* music and the clink of glasses. I was also, I recall, teased about my bad Greek by this peerless poet: 'My dear Larry, your ancient Greek is a music-hall turn, yet funnily enough from some of your poems you seem to

---

* George Seferis (1900–71): Poet and diplomat (Ambassador to London 1957–62). Influenced by French Symbolists and T. S. Eliot, whose poetry he translated into Greek. Nobel Prize 1963.

have understood certain things. But reality is very uncertain with us!' But Paul's postcards were not – they were like pistol-shots – *feux de joie* – and each time I received one in Provence I opened a new bottle of wine and toasted the venture in full confidence!

However the result, it is not for me to judge! Yet luckily enough, I had had time during our meetings to explain myself a little to Paul. Just for the dossier.

I had left school early without apparently showing any particular aptitudes – no desires, except to write poetry and become original if I could. Enough anyway to earn the approval of my parents who were kind people. There had just been time to master the Roman and Greek alphabets so I could limp in Latin and crawl in Greek, but I was widely read in classic paraphrase thanks to Loeb, Oxford, Penguin – I was backward but not completely ignorant. I knew enough to feel that a visit to Greece was a magical event; but I never expected the two images, Greece ancient and modern, to match very closely. The first thing to bowl me over as I sat in a Plaka tavern was not the marble – pearl-ivory-platinum-salt – shadows of the Acropolis at high noon with its blue sky full of seashadow and green lambence – no, it was the beautiful congruence of the shop signs with their notices in great fresh capital letters. But the real shock was that I could read them and construe them. They were all in Greek I knew! I was to discover later that the two languages which have kept this agelessness, this immortality, are Greek and Chinese. All the others have worn out, changed, modified. But Greek had not budged since before Herodotus. Even for Shakespeare nowadays you need a dictionary – after some four centuries. But if today Plato returned in a surprise visit to the old Agora of his native Athens, he would be able to decipher every shop sign – all the graffiti in fact. Bread was still *artos*, wine still *oinos*, and love still *eros* . . . Words out of Plato still doing their everyday jobs in the mouths and minds of the Athenian housewife. Life was still *zoé* and death still *thanatos* and joy *harâ*. These immortal king-symbols were still there large as life, you might say! Suddenly the perennity of the whole country knocked me flat; it became as modern as the latest novel yet older than Jesus. It opened a shutter in my psyche somehow and all the bats flew out of my belfry bearing my first decent poem. The alphabet became as vengefully lovely as the Acropolis marbles waiting for their first despoilers, fully aware that they would outface them with poetry. Poetry!

'What's wrong, dear?' asked my mother anxiously. 'You are looking so pale and inappropriate.'

'Like an omelette with wings!' added my brother helpfully.

'I have just realized something very profound. I have had a sudden flash of realization. Greece is quite unique!'

As a background to this great insight, the tonic heartbeat of the place, so

9

to say, I could hear the rise and fall of Seferis' grave voice reading his poem, and in the even deeper background the steady, pitiless thwacking of a fisherman beating an octopus into eatability. 'Pulse-beats in the mind' as the poet says. The blood pressure of time and stone, the inner music of the spheres. It was wonderful to think that Paul was now embarked on his journey, brush in hand, confronting the same surprises and perplexities and resolving them in colour.

As for poetry, I also have to record my participation in a rare, historic event, namely the march across Athens of the Sacred Legion. They were entraining for the Albanian front – pitifully few, and fully aware that not many of them were likely to see their native Athens again. Old Colonel Gigantes strode at their head with his monocle firmly fixed in place. I was with the Colossus of Maroussi*, George Katsimbalis, who watched the regiment defile with high approbation, growling and stabbing with his huge knobkerrie of a stick with its rubber ferrule. He had done just the same thing – volunteered – in 1914. What amused and delighted him was that the historic 'No' uttered to Italy by General Metaxas set a term to the interminable squabbles and bickerings and jealousies of the Athenian peoples and brought them into line, called them to order, so to speak. Irreconcilable political enemies for half a lifetime suddenly found themselves marching shoulder to shoulder across the Platea Syntagmatos in the white light of morning with the medal of the Sacred Legion on their breasts. I suddenly realized that what was being re-enacted before my eyes was Thermopylae – the Spartan three hundred brought up-to-date. Moreover – for Athens was then only an overgrown village – one recognized among the marching men the faces of so many friends and acquaintances. The Athens bars and taverns had yielded up all their most choice scallywags, tosspots and ne'er-do-wells to join in this sacrifice of arms. The hoarse 'No' of the old General was the tocsin they had been waiting to hear. Without fanfares and drumming the Legion marched in the wonderful morning light into the poetry of death. From another recess of memory comes a snatch of literary gossip, this time from George Katsimbalis – it is not known to everyone that he was a great editor, rather like Cyril Connolly, and he had just come back from London having contacted a then unknown young American poet, T. S. Eliot. Just as Eliot was founding *The Criterion*, George was now busy in Athens founding *Nea Gràmmata* with which he proposed to provide a show-window for the then unknown poet Cavafy† of Alexandria, whose

homosexual love-poems (which had placed him at once in the rank of a modern Theocritus) had given great offence to the puritans of Athens. But George knew his quality and had decided to fight the matter out with a group of new and fiery young writers.

The most flamboyant and magnificent among them was without doubt Angelos Sikelianos* who reigned in the Plaka of the epoch like a sort of Greek D'Annunzio, and his great war-poem ruled the literary roost. It was the most wonderful and pious evocation of what was greeted on all sides as a national event of world significance – which it was: the Greek 'No' and the decision to fight in Albania! The title was so striking that once again I had the shock of reading ancient and modern Greek at once, '*O Nekrō Dêipnos ton Hellenôn*, 'The Corpse-Feast of the Greeks'. Of the five words, all were unchanged since Plato! In its extravagance and the prolixity of its rhetoric, it is still the grand work of art we thought it was then. (I had received my first postcard from an unknown Henry Miller and had sent him a copy!) But George had just had a drink with Sikelianos who had recounted in passing, speaking of his poem, 'But I had to wait for the killing to begin in Albania before beginning my masterpiece. One must exult in everything, it's the only human triumph over death!'

How to express the desperation, indeed perfidiousness of Plaka conviviality during those weeks? The nights so dry and full of flower scents made it an agony to go home to bed. And for those who spent them talking metaphysics with a forever replenished blue wine-jar before them, the night lasted until the sun appeared with a surprised air (as if it was the first time ever) behind the spars of the Acropolis. The sleepy street-cleaners with their hoarse cries of 'Bring out your dead!' (a joke in poor taste nowadays) produced only old Dmitri with his world-famous hangover and his staggering, tottering green wheelbarrow full of empty *ouzo* bottles, still giving off the devilish aniseed-perfume of the Salonika *souks*. As for the *rezina*, it was so fervent and yet so pure that one could pass a whole night drinking it with nothing worse than a spiritual elation and a springy footstep to match the faultless white daybreak! People walked about dazed with wellbeing – 'like consenting adults on shore-leave' as somebody put it, though I am not sure how accurate this is as metaphor. (My family being strictly analphabetic were spared undue cerebration – they behaved as if they were in Lapland.) The blue wine-cans and the whining, pining,

---

* *The Colossus of Maroussi*: Henry Miller's account of his visit to Greece with Durrell in 1939. Katsimbalis is the larger-than-life hero.

† Constantine Cavafy (1863–1933): Worked as a civil servant in Alexandria. Historical memories and personal experiences are inextricably blended in his poetry. His tragic outlook, sensuality and irony reflected contemporary trends in Western culture. He spoke and read English and had a strong influence on both Durrell and E. M. Forster.

* Angelos Sikelianos (1884–1951): Lyric poet and dramatist who tried to combine Greek tradition with Western thought and to introduce the idiom of the people as a consciously literary language.

plaintive scratching of *bouzoukis* playing in concert at nightfall were adjuncts to the fading blue sky; then the first soft call of the Athenian owls. Even they had not changed – I suppose because they were under the personal protection of the Goddess Athena!

But by now my colleague and collaborator had set out on a further leg of his journey and was brooding on another landscape which lacked the Venetian atmospheres of Corfu and Zante and produced in their place the thrilling and solemn diapason of Crete with her white cliffs a-dazzle. Here he must have run into some perplexities, to have been momentarily discountenanced by the philosophical challenges – for Crete seems to resume the whole childhood of Metaphysics and Mathematics. The ancient labyrinth still holds out promises unfulfilled like the origins of the alphabet, say, the source of numbers, and so many kindred puzzles of history. But the key has been thrown away. Yet the basic landscapes are of vast felicity of rhythm and coherence and almost compensate for the heartbreak in not being able to penetrate the island's major secrets. In the modern pantheon, however, Crete stands for the unforgiving splendour of penury and valour – it's a small Scotland in its rocky, aristocratic self-possession. Poet's country – and a country of poets with its own Greek pronounced with a characteristic slanting twang. But my own visual memories concerning Crete have always been marked by an ancient one of a Cretan regiment walking through a village on their way to the harbour, bound for Egypt. The black and white rocks had burst out in a wild splendour of crimson and white roses which the girls had plucked to stop the rifles of the soldiers. It was amazing in its beauty, the regiment moving down to the blue harbour waters like a flower bed with its rose-stopped guns. We dreamed of roses for a whole season, my painter wife and I, and grew desperate trying to bring our water-colours to bear on this thrilling subject-matter – in vain. The topic grew more and more metaphysical in the course of our discussions, and much later on when I took a pseudonym and started to paint myself I took a few hints from a gnostic friend called Epfs on the whole matter, and jotted down his *obiter dicta* in my notebook:

'To deal truthfully with the matter you must first paint the rose in its physical form as pure flower. Next forget the physical form and paint the perfume. Next forget everything and paint the idea of the rose, a rose, any rose. Aim for the Jackpot. Tell yourself that the rose after all was not created by nature but by man – a compilation of tensions like a wine or a water-colour. Once you become a real painter you realise that everything about it is strictly imaginary except the thorns.' (Adapted from a Sufi mystic).

Crete, the Penniless Princess of the Cyclades, is one of the many poetical sites where the insight of the medieval bards pitched an altar, a temple for the Holy Grail. The Rose of Poetic insight flourished there.

Modern Crete carries so many of these cross-references built into the structure of its way-of-life that you feel suddenly you are in a world whose bard is Mistral or Walter Scott. About Cretan pride I can provide a number of text-book evocations, but one will do. Once at a village bus-stop on the high road from Chanea, we were stopped by a flock of sheep – rather, by its irascible shepherd. During this brief halt, my eye took in a highly significant scene being enacted on a vine-shaded terrace overlooking the sea. The chief actor was a little old lady, quite withered up like a crab-apple, but of a supreme, indeed quite intimidating dignity of dress (her Sunday best, which for the island means black snood and shawls somewhat like those of Arles during the Spring Feria). You know how it is – sometimes in a single brief flash one can take in a whole scene and grasp its meaning almost instantaneously. This is what happened during the brief altercation between the villager and our bus driver.

It was obvious – you could discern it from the relative facial expressions – that the old lady in all the full splendour of her poverty was selling her last treasure, the little stone house with its snatch of land and half-dozen olive trees. Her grief was invisible, yet somehow her pride of posture conveyed the tragic sense of the situation. Obviously the family was bankrupt save for these last possessions. But the buyers were a couple of suave yokels, promoters in town dress with dreadful hats and manners, vulgar and pushy products of small town life. This was the final discussion before signing the deed of sale. Obviously this little old mountain lady, who looked so like the Queen of Mycenae, would have to make her mark, for she could not write. But her sublime insolence of carriage and her contemptuous regard for the two promoters stamped her as a natural aristocrat in terms of human values. It was so obvious that the two promoters were athirst to obtain the little property in order to cut down all the trees and plant a dozen foul, ugly villas for sale to townees like themselves. The contract lay on a side-table apart under an ancient brass candlestick with the candle which would be lit for the actual ceremony. But what was so arresting was that she had emerged from the one-room little house with a tray and glasses backed by a flagon which must once have held Cretan *ouzo. But it was empty!*

The laws of island hospitality are quite inflexible and must at all costs be honoured. But – even the promoters were touched and abashed by so grievous a social situation – there was not a drop of drink in the house with which to honour the deed of sale in traditional style. The old girl, however, lit the candle. She had all the masterful, unerring nonchalance of being sure of her station, her place in nature. Everyone held his breath uncertain of what might evolve out of such an intangible and ambiguous situation. And also from pity for her, even the horrible townee promoters had a gleam of sympathy in their minds. But her resolution and behaviour were proof against every shortcoming; they burned as uprightly as her candle. She took up the *ouzo*-flagon and with unfaltering, expressionless simplicity poured out a dose of – nothingness – into each glass before handing the tray round.

The perfection of her mien and her address – they were overwhelming: it was clearly not possible to disobey the rules. They must be mimed, so each of her guests took his seat and drank off a couple of imaginary sips of formal *ouzo* – pure air! – even going as far as to modestly smack his lips (or pretend to) with appreciation of this delicious home-brewed alcohol. This little dramatic mime was performed with sincerity and feeling by all. Then the glasses were replaced on the tray and they fell to business – I suppose haggling over the price. But I could see no more, for the bus gave a lurch forward and we were at once enveloped in a cloud of scented dust thrown up by the sheep – overpowering scent of oranges and tangerines. The little scene remained engraven in my thoughts as something very typical of Crete. I still treasure it as an example of high style.

Paul Hogarth in his vertiginous journey must have had a dozen such cameos of daily life presented to his alert and vivacious eye: presented and then swept away by something as ordinary as the lurch of a bus. And, of course, for the painter the visual reality of the place – even if it was a vast banquet of forms and colours – presented all the old intractable philosophic problems thrown up by the contemporary slant of science which had put a question-mark over the whole range of circumstantial transactions relating to time and space as functions of truth. After all, the artist was supposed to be a dealer in truth – it was his working capital, so to speak. But . . . suddenly to be informed that all truth was highly provisional, and that there was no such thing as a stable fact in all nature because simply by observing a field you disturbed it. Your reports on nature were only marginally correct. The old stable world-view where mind and matter played supporting roles in perfect truthful integration was no longer a truth. Reality had fallen to bits under the poet's regard and his poems were trying to bear witness to it.

Reality had turned rebel and the shock of the impact had actually disturbed syntax – hence the quite outrageous thought-formations of the Surrealists and others like Gertrude Stein, the babble queen with her ever-repeated poem insisting that *a rose is a rose is a rose* – it sounded such rubbish! It bore witness to the distress which was now afflicting philosophic thought. The new thought – the new relativity principle – had disturbed syntax – by which I mean the classical structure of statement which consisted of subject and object with a verb in the middle as a motor, a heartbeat. This linearity of statement was compromised when it came to making a poetic statement, and apparent chaos was the result. How to sort the whole matter out? The poet was tentatively trying to suggest that we should feast on the discord and try to coax a new truth from it – a new sensibility might come into being from this way of seeing (Picasso?). Art was echoing this distress with manifestations like atonal music and, in painting, Cubism! Also Seferis with his original 'tangential' style was representative of the new orientation. His poems were like nudges, little nuggets of insight. A poetry of weird collisions and tensions was coming into being. Even straight matter under the huge punch of nuclear fission had obligingly disintegrated and offered a recipe for great disturbances in the form of bombs . . . (Let us hope these mischievous attainments remain in the limbo of the Gods and do not realize themselves in destructive ways!)

But the most disconcerting fact of the new thought for the philosophic tourist was the dissolution of the old stable personality, the fictive ego quite separate and discrete and apart. In the new reality which was so highly provisional, it had turned into something else which seemed to resemble an Indian notion of being, under which time was extended and your being consisted of a congeries of attributes merely. 'You' consisted of your mother's smile, father's eyes, daughter's laugh, grandfather's aptitude for chess or sex or cookery . . . one biography with endless facets. 'You' was a figment. The new equation said that you were one soul using up numberless different bodies – houses of flesh in which to let countless historical situations evolve through thousands of coefficients of a numinous value. As the Indian poet has it,

> You can set sail by simply sitting still,
> Pour out the silence and Poets will drink their fill;
> The Principle of Indeterminacy
> Will grease the mighty cogs of Will.

There is no more appropriate place to nourish these perplexities which rule modern life than a Cretan tavern with a view over the harbour – for Crete is the spiritual turntable which awaits the tourist who is the least bit awake to the historical nuances underlined by – to take the most dramatic example – the extinct volcano of Santorini at whose terrifying crater you can pause today, discountenanced by this hole blown in the side of nature, desolate beyond belief and yet exhilarating: the din must have been unbearable as the sea rushed in with a tidal wave which almost carried away the moon; it must have seemed that way to the few survivors of this historic calamity: that is to say, if there were any. Of the two great earthquakes about which we have a few scraps of viable information, the second which arrived around 1400 to 1450 BC seems to have been definitive, to have carried away every trace of the flourishing thalasocracy, the culture of Crete which had penetrated to every corner of the known world thanks to the sea-communications opened up by the merchant fleets of the island.

Recent scholarship concerned with the culture of the Aegean has pushed the identification about as far as it can go in urging upon us the Atlantis history as described in Plato's version of the Critias – as fact, historical fact; in which case we have a well authenticated version of the natural calamity on a scale which beggars all description. We should not forget that Plato was in a position to profit from the gossip of historians as much as anyone because he was widely travelled and as a *négociant* in olive-oil must have kept a sharp eye out for scholars and poets to offer him illustrations to his own impressions and intuitions.

I think he would have offered a warmly sympathetic welcome to the angle of inclination in much modern scholarship, which some find too adventurous. I am thinking of the lectures of scholars like J. G. Bennet (*New Light on Atlantis*, 1962) and Dr Galanopoulos of Athens University whose brilliant detective work was the first to adopt radio-carbon dating to the volcanic ash, which enabled him to offer some tentative precisions about the critical date which swept everything overboard: so that it makes a plausible point of departure for our own history to gradually take shape. Of course there are still whole areas of darkness; it is inevitable when one is dealing with such vast slabs of time. But Hogarth's instinct to start his voyage of discovery with the desolate chasm of Santorini was an admirable decision – the whole of Galanopoulos' closely and plausibly argued theses about the submarine volcano make excellent sense for our scholars today. It has been estimated by other scientists that the force of such an explosion could be calculated tentatively as exceeding that of somewhat more than the simultaneous discharge of 430 Hydrogen Bombs of full calibre! Imagine!

But I am not present to qualify anything in this exquisite *bonbonnière* of a book – so rich in its implications. All the echoes are faithfully present, and the whole is held together by the fine tensions of an artist who recognizes that good art should convey a slight touch of the unbearable, of menace under felicity.

For me especially it is richly evocative of a prolonged journey I once took in the hope of catching a glimpse of the famous black roses of Rhodes, an island originally named after its famous roses; but I failed in my quest (I was planning a book about the Dodecanese islands which might historically illustrate how ancient Greek temples gradually evolved into Christian churches, and finally cathedrals). Alas! my scholarship let me down, though I came to the conclusion that this cryptic black rose was the Crusaders' rose, which became representative of the rose of the Initiates, the rose of Intuition: The Grail!

This is no place to drag Homeric issues into the bull-ring but I was, of course, reminded all the time that Homer's favourite adjective was 'rose-fingered' when it came to referring to the sunrise, and anyone who has watched it from sea or land in Lindos or Cameiros will at once be struck by the appositeness – as if he had been plunged back into his own Stone Age memories. Paul Hogarth's colour-box has done the memory proud. But this is the place to leave him to speak for himself. It's with a profound sense of gratitude I do so now. What memories –

And what an adventure!   **Lawrence Durrell**

ELISE AT NIMES

Promontaries shaven to the skull,
A wind to pluck the teeth from your head!
We camped somewhere between the living and the dead,
Like wet moles in the frozen ruck-scrub.
The fierce slang of the dawn rain described
Its scolding monotony of fallen drops –
Rigour and precision of that last night when
You told me how a picture by Turner
Upset your reason and digestion by its
Unexpected force of vision: adding that art
Should do just that, outrage and disturb,
Not just contrive and move but really punish!
Dawn came and you left, and now you say
You are heading for the USA
To learn our lingo. Start with Okay, honey,
It will get you anywhere, just okay, okay.
Your fine French kisses with the news they bore
Made everything a spice, precious as lace,
Risky, soft and rife as mice. They wore
Felicity after too much emptiness. Later in the war,
The great adventure with words, you'll find
The greatest beauties to be accidental for
The top felicity is always involuntary like
Saying 'Intensive Care Unit' for someone
Knocked breathless by an unexpected love.

13

PROSPERO'S CELL

CORFU IS PRESENTED WITH THE INTIMATE DETAIL THAT ONLY A RESIDENT CAN ACQUIRE. LAWRENCE DURRELL LIVED THERE FOR FIVE YEARS BEFORE THE WAR. THE RESULT IS NOT A TRAVELOGUE BUT A POETIC REMINISCENCE SALTED WITH THE SADNESS OF TIME REMEMBERED. 'SEEN THROUGH THE TRANSFORMING LENS OF MEMORY THE PAST SEEMED SO ENCHANTED THAT EVEN THOUGHT WOULD BE UNWORTHY OF IT.' THE INESCAPABLE LURE OF THE ISLAND IS MADE REAL THROUGH ACCOUNTS OF THE ADVENTURE OF DAY-TO-DAY LIVING, AND ITS PAST, FABULOUS AND HISTORICAL, EMERGES THROUGH CONVERSATIONS AMONG AN INTIMATE CIRCLE OF FRIENDS — THE COUNT D WISTFULLY SUGGESTS THAT IT IS PROSPERO'S ISLE IN 'THE TEMPEST' (AFTER ALL, 'SYCORAX' IS ALMOST AN ANAGRAM FOR ITS LATIN NAME, 'CORCYRA'), THEODORE STEPHANIDES PRODUCES HIS SHOEMAKER, ISCARIOTES, TO SUPPORT THE THEORY THAT JUDAS HAD CONNECTIONS THERE AND ZARIAN ADDS A METAPHYSICAL NOTE BY CLAIMING THAT THE LANDSCAPE 'PRECIPITATES THE INWARD CRISIS OF LIVES AS YET NOT FULLY WORKED OUT'. THE QUEST TO DISCOVER THE BEACH WHERE ULYSSES MET NAUSICAA IS LEAVENED WITH EXAMPLES OF THE BRITISH LEGACY: CRICKET AND THE 'ENGLISH' HOUSE — A HOUSE WITH A LAVATORY AND EVEN, PERHAPS (UNHEARD OF, AND TO THE PEASANTS UNNECESSARY) A BATHROOM.

LAWRENCE DURRELL'S COMMENT: The travel books are interspersed between the novels because the time spent on their research provided a respite from the creative energy demanded by the novels. They are 'breathers' between bouts of total involvement.

St Spiridion
'Here in the church of St Spiridion, Venice and Turkey compete in silver and brass, in bronze and iron; and under this tortured inlay-work and colour the dark pagan eyes still stare with their fleshly hunger – reminding you how close the old pantheon is, locked in this narrow ritualism.'

L D:
The festivals associated with the Saint were animated by children and became a sort of *commedia dell'arte*.

The Old Fort, Corfu Town
'Lithgow published an account of Corfu in 1632. It is as follows: "The City Corfu, from which the Ile hath its name, is situated at the foot of a Mountain whereupon are builded two strong fortresses, and invironed with a rock. The one is called Fortezza Nova and the other Fortezza Vecchia. They are well governed and circumspectly kept, lest by the instigation of the one Captain the other should commit any treasonable effect . . . The Castels are inaccesable and unconquerable, if that the keepers be loyal, and provided with natural and martial furniture." '

15

The Achilleion
'A monstrous building surrounded
by gimcrack sculptures and lovely
gardens belonging to the late
Kaiser.'

Palace of St Michael and St George

L D:
A symbol of the British raj but a friendly
one, not aggressive. It is significant that
cricket was played on the *maidan* in front of it.

17

SUMMER IN CORFU

At last the serious days of summer
When from the red forge dancing,
The blacksmith sunshine hammers
New beaks for the flesh.
From the black mint
Steel for new flint.

State me no theme for misery. The season
Like a woman lies open, is folding,
Secret, growth upon growth. The black fig,
Desire, is torn again from the belly of Reason.
Our summer is gravid at last, is big.

All you, who know desire in these seas,
Have souls or equipment for loneliness, loneliness,
Lean now like fruitage. The Hesperides
Open. This is the limbo, the doldrum.
Seal down the eye of your cyclops,
Silence time's drum.

The White House, Kalamai
'It is April and we have taken an old
fisherman's house in the extreme
north of the island – Kalamai. Ten
sea-miles from the town, and some
thirty kilometres by road, it offers
all the charms of seclusion. A white
house set like a dice on a rock
already venerable with the scars of
wind and water. The hill runs clear
up into the sky behind it, so that the
cypresses and olives overhang this
room in which I sit and write. We
are upon a bare promontory with its
beautiful clean surface of
metamorphic stone covered in olive
and ilex: in the shape of a *mons
pubis*. This is become our
unregretted home. A world.
Corcyra.'

L D:
Living here introduced Durrell to a simple
life uncluttered by the paraphernalia of
civilization. Life was basic – a few eating
utensils, water from a pump, an outside
water closet but electricity generated by its
own miniature windmill. It was a spartan
way of life which was much favoured by
Greek writers. The spirit of Greece is
perhaps epitomized by frugality. The
beauty of the natural surroundings
emphasized by the brilliant sunlight is
pristine and does not need modern
comforts to make it congenial.

The Artist's Journal

Edward Lear, if recalled from his niche in a heavenly Hall of Fame, would probably insist on returning there forthwith after seeing what has happened to his beloved Corfu. His water-colour drawing of the view of Garitsa Bay from Kanóni Point with the islets of Pondikonissi and Vlaherna, is one of his most poetic images of the Eden that was nineteenth-century Corfu. Today, the graceless bulk of an enormous Hilton dominates a coastline jammed with cheap hotels, fast-food eateries, bars and discos. The islets with their monasteries look as if they really shouldn't be there at all.

Yet there is much to draw. In Corfu Town there's the Old Fort with its Venetian overtones. Cartouches and crenellated turrets, cannon and angled ramparts appeal to the heart and mind of the artist-traveller and I make the most of them. Nearby, the Palace of St Michael and St George strikes a British note. Formerly the residence and headquarters of the High Commissioners, it looks like a bit of Bath that has somehow gone astray.

As I pursue my quest for places described by the maestro, frustration alternates with pleasure. I am anxious to visit the estate of Count D. But an old friend of Durrell's, Maria Aspiotti, tells me that 'Count D' is not one person but a composite of three, whose names (Maria was a member of the Greek Resistance movement during World War II) she will not reveal. Moreover, the 'Count's estate' was not in the Valley di Ropa but near Vatsos on the western side of the island. And as the grape harvest has already taken place there is really little point in my going there. More bad news follows. A prime Durrell haunt in Corfu Town, 'The Sign of the Partridge' taverna is now a boutique. As if to offer me a consolation prize, Maria adds that the old fisherman's house where he lived with Nancy from 1936 to 1938, survives as the White Taverna; a modest establishment which lets its rooms to the more impecunious foreign visitor.

The next day I drive to Kalamai, some thirty kilometres to the north. And there, at the end of a quiet picturesque bay overshadowed by a thickly wooded mountainside, I see the old house; its original character unexpectedly intact as it is closed for the winter. Not a soul is about as I draw.

The Palace of Achilleion, built in 1892 by Elisabeth, the beautiful headstrong Empress of Austria, as a retreat from the intrigues of the Hapsburg Court, was dismissed by Larry as 'monstrous'. But I find its groves of darkling pine and cypress evoke a haunted classicism, reminiscent of the unquiet art of the Swiss painter Arnold Böcklin. But not for long, as it is very much a tourist attraction. While teenagers inscribe messages on cacti, adults simulate the postures of antique statues to the raucous encouragement of their companions.

THE DARK LABYRINTH

THE MYSTERY AND MENACE OF THE CENTRAL SITUATION, ENTOMBMENT IN THE LABYRINTH, IS A PARABLE ON POST-WAR PRIORITIES AND INDIVIDUAL VALUES. DURING THE WAR THE LABYRINTH SUSTAINED A BAND OF GUERILLAS FIGHTING AGAINST NAZI OPPRESSION, BUT ONCE THE WAR IS OVER IT BECOMES A TESTING GROUND FOR SPIRITUAL STRENGTH IN AN UNREGENERATE WORLD. ITS GUARDIANS ARE A POLYGLOT ARCHAEOLOGIST AND A GREEK ABBOT WHO LIVE IN CEFALÛ AND A MONASTERY NEARBY. A MOTLEY GROUP OF TOURISTS ARE ASSEMBLED TO FACE THE LABYRINTH'S CHALLENGE. THE TWO WHO KNOW IT BEST ESCAPE THE ORDEAL; ONE IS REJECTED BECAUSE OF HIS INTELLECTUAL TIMIDITY, THE OTHER FINDS REFUGE IN A FALSE MIRACLE. A MISSIONARY FAILS THE TEST BECAUSE SHE CANNOT FACE THE REALITY OF WHAT SHE HAS BEEN TEACHING ALL HER LIFE, AND A MEDIUM IS DEVOURED BY HIS OWN MIASMA. A PAINTER PROVES HIMSELF AS AN ARTIST BUT ONLY ACHIEVES FULFILMENT AS A MAN BY SACRIFICING HIMSELF TO SAVE A CALLOW TYPIST WHO IS RETURNED TO THE WORLD WOUNDED BY THE EXPERIENCE. ONLY A HAPPY, ORDINARY COUPLE (THE PURE IN HEART) TRANSCEND THE TRAUMA AND ATTAIN A NEW EDEN. THE LABYRINTH, FOR ALL ITS DRAMATIC DETAIL, IS AN EMBLEM SET IN THE IDYLLIC REALITY OF CRETE.

LAWRENCE DURRELL'S COMMENT: The classical association with the Minotaur and the Labyrinth accounts for Crete being chosen as the setting since it adds another dimension to the genre of the spy-story. There were already many expert writers in the field; one had to look to one's laurels.

The Entrance to the Labyrinth
'At first they hesitated, so narrow and uninviting was the entrance – a single corridor of orange-red rock which took a steep turn after five paces and passed out of sight. "It is little bigger than an Egyptian rock-tomb," said Graecen fretfully, as he turned up the collar of his coat and felt for his torch. The guide turned back and beckoned. "Plenty light inside," he shouted encouragingly and disappeared. They followed him one by one. "Not too fast," said Campion, as they entered the stone cave and heard the church bell of Cefalû become suddenly very distant, and then at last smother out in the subterranean roar and splash of a spring hammering on rock.'

20

Cefalû, near Chanea

'He looked back once more at Cefalû and caught his breath. It was a fantastic locality; a huge cone of conglomerate rising a thousand feet into the blue Cretan air. On the one side it ran clear up from the sea as if it had been sheared out by some insane architect. The sides were weathered and lightly covered in holm-oak and myrtle. On the very crown rose a tuft of green cypresses and olives. Half-way up the cone stood the village of Cefalû, its houses with their child's paint-box colours glowing pristine and ingenuous in the waning sunlight. The mountain ran straight up from this little circle of cultivation, into the sky. He could see the avenue of small cypresses that led to the mouth of the labyrinth. Then, below the road, he could look down to the lovely house that Axelos had called Cefalû. It was built in a fault of the rock which gave it access to the sea. A white sailing boat lay like a breathing butterfly against the white mole.'

21

Old Chanea

The Monastery of St George
'He was almost down to the sea-line again as he skirted the cliff-path above St George. Below him, perched on the irregular hill-side he could see the red belfry and the white wall of the monastery glowing in the light of the afternoon sun. It had been built at a point where a shallow stream made an issue through the rock to reach the sea. Thus, in all that wild landscape it seemed to be an oasis of greenery, for the fresh water had thrown up cherry and walnut trees to cluster about it. Seen from above, the little building seemed to float upon this dense green sheet of foliage.'

Aptera with White Mountains
'The cars had blundered over the dusty part of the road, and now their tyres crunched on the pot-holed surfaces of the mountain roads. They had mounted the first three gradients which led slowly along the first escarpments of the White Mountains. The road wound in and out of several frowning ravines, where white torrents broke from the parapets of rock, and the air was full of the cries of swifts. It had become purer and more limpid, and the atmosphere colder. They were glad of their coats.'

L D:
The wildlife of eagles and buzzards complements the sense of space and solitude. Crete is a forbidding island, and the strength of the sunlight enhances the air of mystery, a pervasive feeling of foreboding.

The Artist's Journal

The White Mountains

'They walked down into the little valley, hand in hand, looking about them curiously. The prospect looked, with all its cultivation, like the park of some great house – the result of deliberate labour and intention rather than the casual handiwork of Nature. A stream blundered over gravel. Birds sang. A walnut tree nodded its pronged branches in the wind. Farther down beyond the last bluff of rock, puffs of colour stood out against the grey hills – peach-blossom. Warm, verdant, and unself-conscious the meadows seemed to have been tended and mown, lying in the shadow of the sun-burnt mountains. They were filled with a gradually growing sense of incredulity and amazement, comparing the richness of the amphitheatre in which they stood with the brooding hulks of stone which raised themselves in the air at every point. Their feet trod grass. Yet everywhere they turned their eyes picked up the formidable crests of mountains plunged in snow. "I can't make it out," he said slowly, "it seems queer somehow. It's so warm." His wife walked silently beside him tasting the purity of the air as it entered her lungs and was expelled from them. The mountains looked grandiose and beautiful rather than menacing. She was full of that light-headedness which comes upon all who walk upon the mountains of Greece, and feel the scent of thyme mingling with the pure cold air.'

L D:
Crete evokes an atmosphere of isolation which made it possible to set 'the new Eden' in the White Mountains where the constant mist adds to the sense of unreality, dissolving and reappearing like a film sequence. It is easy to imagine getting lost there.

Security restrictions inhibit the artist-traveller of today no less than in the nineteenth century. The adventurous pencil of the topographical water-colourist and the Special Artist was then the sole means of gathering pictorial information. Apparently, we still remain a threat. Durrell's eloquent description of the grandeur of Suda Bay suggests I attempt a seascape. I drive about the area, only to find it is now dominated by a huge NATO naval base, prohibited to the unauthorized visitor. Signs announce that the taking of pictures by *any* means is strictly forbidden. I drive on to the site of ancient Aptera and from an abandoned Turkish fort depict the remains of this once great Graeco-Roman city state against the distant escarpments of the White Mountains.

Durrell's Cefalû of *The Dark Labyrinth* is, in fact, present-day Kefalas. I have also succeeded in identifying the Monastery of St George which, I'm told, is near Karvadi *en route* to Kefalas. I lose my way several times. But eventually I find the monastery nestling on a rocky hillside overlooking a vast and verdant valley with a glimpse of the sea in the distance. I can't be sure that it really was the place that Larry had in mind. In the mellow light of the afternoon sun, the old monastery possesses enough of a haunted ambience to persuade me that I should depict what remains of its bygone splendour. Kefalas itself, however, presents a different problem. I'm halfway down a vertiginous mountain road before I realize that Durrell must have seen the village from sea level, obviously from a boat. The sun beats down as I squint up at the 'fantastic cone of conglomerate' to which the village clings. But the village has disappeared. I have to retrace my steps in order to add its 'houses with their child's-paint-box-colours'.

Crete is indeed a picturesque land, but a great deal of trouble has to be taken to find suitable vantage points from which to draw it. In this respect, Edward Lear had the advantage of making his way about the island on horseback, staying close to the country in nearby inns, and rising at the crack of dawn to catch the charismatic rays of first light. By the time I arrive on the scene, swiftly moving clouds have reduced visibility but I persevere and finally make a passable view of the White Mountains near Kaina.

I spend a further two days drawing in Chanea, a somewhat sad city, which looks to its past with nostalgia and regret. The old merchant district to the east of the Outer Harbour is crowded with fine old Venetian and Turkish houses with balconies and richly ornamented porticoes. Many are being restored as night-clubs and hotels, but most remain as warren-like tenements where the tide of life, in Dr Johnson's words, is fullest. People quarrel, shout and fight with one another against a cacophony of cries from passing pedlars and yelping dogs.

REFLECTIONS ON A MARINE VENUS

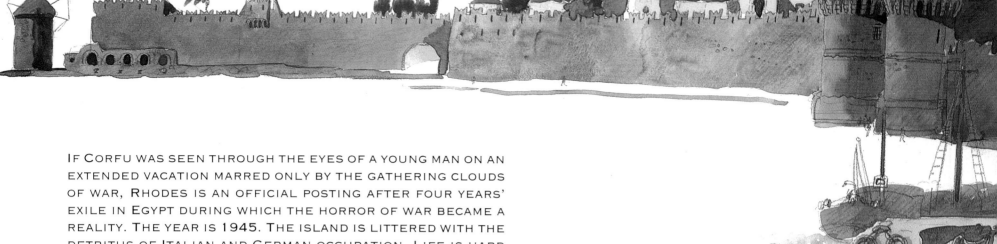

IF CORFU WAS SEEN THROUGH THE EYES OF A YOUNG MAN ON AN EXTENDED VACATION MARRED ONLY BY THE GATHERING CLOUDS OF WAR, RHODES IS AN OFFICIAL POSTING AFTER FOUR YEARS' EXILE IN EGYPT DURING WHICH THE HORROR OF WAR BECAME A REALITY. THE YEAR IS 1945. THE ISLAND IS LITTERED WITH THE DETRITUS OF ITALIAN AND GERMAN OCCUPATION. LIFE IS HARD FOR THE INHABITANTS AND UNSTABLE FOR THE LIBERATORS. THROUGH THE PAINFUL PROCESS OF A RETURN TO PEACE, DURRELL'S ZEST FOR LIFE AND LOVE FOR THE ISLANDS ASSERT THEMSELVES. HE COLLECTS ANOTHER CIRCLE OF FRIENDS JUST AS ECCENTRIC IF LESS UPROARIOUS. TOGETHER THEY SHARE THEIR PASSION FOR THE PAST — THE HISTORY OF THE COLOSSUS AND OF THE KNIGHTS OF ST JOHN — AND THEIR APPRECIATION OF THE ENDURING PRESENT. 'IN RHODES THE DAYS DROP AS SOFTLY AS FRUIT FROM TREES.' IN THIS HIATUS, THOUGHTS ARE GERMINATING WHICH WILL CULMINATE IN **THE ALEXANDRIA QUARTET**: 'ISOLATED MOMENTS EXISTING IN A PECULIAR DENSE MEDIUM OF THEIR OWN WHICH WAS LIKE TIME BUT NOT OF IT. EACH MOMENT TO ITSELF ENTIRE, POPULATING A WHOLE CONTINUUM OF FEELING . . .' AND 'IN THE BLITHE AIR OF RHODES SHE (THE MARINE VENUS) HAS PROVIDED US WITH A VICARIOUS SENSE OF CONTINUITY NOT ONLY WITH THE PAST — BUT ALSO WITH THE FUTURE — FOR SURELY HISTORY'S EVALUATIONS ARE WRONG IN SPEAKING OF CIVILIZED AND BARBARIC AGES SUCCEEDING OR PRECEDING ONE ANOTHER, SURELY THEY HAVE ALWAYS CO-EXISTED — FOR ONE IS THE MEASURE OF THE OTHER? EVERYWHERE THE DUALISM OF THE HUMAN PERSONALITY HAS CREATED SIDE BY SIDE PROFANITY AND PIETY, TRUTH AND FALSEHOOD, HATE AND LOVE.'

Rhodes old town
'Below us in the great amphitheatre where once the white city of Hippodamus lay, with its sacred groves and temples, its dazzling statuary and teeming dock-yards, the Crusader town lours, with its gross bastions and keeps shining through the evening mist, topped by the minarets and the turning windmills of the Turkish quarter.'

LAWRENCE DURRELL'S COMMENT:
The painting recalls an eighteenth-century engraving, which is entirely appropriate to the town.

Argyrokastrou Square, Rhodes old town

L D:
In 1945, after he had left Egypt, Lawrence Durrell was appointed Public Information Officer and had his HQ in the building on the right, the Armeria Palace, where he edited newspapers in three languages. Two colleagues were Eve Cohen and Spiro's son. Spiro is the main Corfiot character in both Lawrence Durrell's *Prospero's Cell* and his brother Gerald's *My Family and Other Animals*. During the German Occupation, his son acted as interpreter in the interrogation of the captured British Commandos who have figured so prominently in Kurt Waldheim's history. He considers that Waldheim acted only in the normal capacity of a junior officer.

The Street of Knights, Rhodes old town
'Then we pursued our way across the deserted market-place and entered the old walled town of the Crusaders, passing by the lovely and undamaged gothic tower of St Paul. At the spur of a gentle incline we turned into the famous Street of the Knights at the top of which lay the Castello – that monument to bad taste executed by the latest Italian governor.'

L D:
It was a dead quarter of the town, a monument to the past, and needed a recurrent fair to fill it with people and so bring it back to life. Although some fairs did take place, for instance, one for the celebration and sale of figs, they were not built into the calendar like religious festivals. The British should have stayed on in Rhodes after the War for a few more years in order to stabilize the agronomy.
They left when nothing had been satisfactorily decided. The Brigadier, who was also the civil governor, conducted Durrell's marriage to Eve Cohen, who till then had been a stateless person. It was the day he left the island for good.

31

IN THE GARDEN: VILLA CLEOBOLUS

The mixtures of this garden
Conduct at night the pine and oleander,
Perhaps married to dust's thin edge
Or lime where the cork-tree rubs
The quiet house, bruising the wall:

And dense the block of thrush's notes
Press like a bulb and keeping time
In this exposure to the leaves,
And as we wait the servant comes,

A candle shielded in the warm
Coarse coral of her hand, she weaves
A pathway for her in the golden leaves,
Gathers the books and ashtrays in her arm
Walking towards the lighted house,

Brings with her from the uninhabited
Frontiers of the darkness to the known
Table and tree and chair
Some half-remembered passage from a fugue
Played from some neighbour's garden
On an old horn-gramophone,

And you think: if given once
Authority over the word,
Then how to capture, praise or measure
The full round of this simple garden,
All its nonchalance at being,
How to adopt and raise its pleasure?

Press as on a plate this observed
And simple shape, like wine?
And from the many undeserved
Tastes of the mouth select the crude
Flavour of fruit in pottery
Coloured among this lovely neighbourhood?

Beyond, I mean, this treasure hunt
Of selves, the pains we sort to be
Confined within the loving chamber of a form,
Within a poem locked and launched
Along the hairline of the normal mind?

Perhaps not this: but somehow, yes,
To outflank the personal neurasthenia
That lies beyond in each expiring kiss:
Bring joy, as lustrous on this dish
The painted dancers motionless in play
Spin for eternity, describing for us all
The natural history of the human wish.

Villa Cleobolus, Rhodes new town

The Mosque of Murad Reis
'It was now, I remember, that we stumbled upon the little garden which encircles the Mosque of Murad Reis – a garden at whose heart I was later to find the Villa Cleobolus; and here we sat for a while perched upon Turkish tombstones, smoking and enjoying the darkness which had now (spring was advanced) an almost touchable smoothness, the silkiness of old velours.'

The Artist's Journal

Lindos Bay from the Acropolis
'The configurations of the promontory upon which the town is built suggest something like the talons of the crab. The little harbour is all but land-locked and the blue of it drenches you like spray. The beach-shallows are picked out in lime-green and yellow, against the reddish, deckle-edged surfaces of stone. In the air above it rides the acropolis. It does not insist. It can afford not to presume, so certain of the impact which it must make on everyone who comes upon it through the gulley in the rock. Is not Lindos the official beauty-spot of Rhodes?'

Rhodes, arguably the loveliest of the islands of the eastern Mediterranean, much resembles Majorca in the degree of its verdant lushness. Like Palma, the character of Rhodes Old Town is magically medieval. Gate towers and crenellated palaces from the era of the Crusades dominate the skyline of the walled city, broken here and there by the accent of a mosque's minarets from the days of the Ottoman Empire. You are back in the world of the Knights of St John. Yet, I find it hard to suppress the feeling that I am in a theme-park. In Argyrokastrou Square, where Durrell had his office in the Almeria Palace (when he simultaneously edited three newspapers in Greek, Italian and Turkish), and in the cobbled Street of the Knights, one expects Charlton Heston suddenly to appear on stage and leap from a window or rampart, sword and buckler in hand.

Elsewhere, such impressions blur. When I first read *Reflections on a Marine Venus*, I succumbed, like many a reader, to the introspective mood Durrell evoked in his description of his days on Rhodes. Now I have to find the visual equations to match his reflective prose. A difficult task indeed. After the Old Town, I discover the graveyard of the Mosque of Murad Reis, whose tombs, to quote Durrell, resemble 'huge mushrooms . . . ineffable decay like a Christina Rossetti peytol trance'. As I draw, an old crone mutters unintelligibly, indeed like a figure from an illustration for a poem in a Victorian literary magazine. Nearby is the tiny studio house which Larry dubbed the Villa Cleobolus (after the genial tyrant, a native of Rhodes and allegedly one of the seven wise men of antiquity) and rented as his workroom. The little studio is now occupied by the caretaker of the cemetery, and still very much 'buried by flowering hibiscus'. It was built during the regime of the enlightened governor Mario Lago (Rhodes was an Italian colony, 1912–45) in the fashionable Art Deco style as part of a grand design for a desirable enclave for wealthy businessmen and colonial officials.

But there is much more to Rhodes than a heavily restored medieval town or even the Turkish past. *En route* to Lindos I pass through the villages of Archangelos and Malonas. The former is run by women. They own the land and till the soil while their menfolk drink *ouzo* in the cafés. Stout women in kerchiefs with huge calves and bobby socks swagger down the main street after working in the fields. As I rapidly make a sketch, one such Amazon, hoe in hand, advances on me with knitted brows. I decide that evasion is the better part of valour and drive on to Malonas just a few kilometres away, where the men are back in the saddle. Malonas is also full of ancient unpainted stone houses somewhat Turkish in style, although they display carved crucifixes above their front doors.

WHITE EAGLES OVER SERBIA

THIS BOOK IS IN THE TRADITION OF JOHN BUCHAN'S ADVENTURE STORIES. COLONEL METHUEN, AN ARCHETYPAL ENGLISH HERO, IS SENT ON A SECRET MISSION TO YUGOSLAVIA. HE BECOMES INVOLVED WITH ROYALIST PARTISANS WHO ARE TRYING TO TAKE HIDDEN TREASURE OUT OF THE COUNTRY. THE DRABNESS OF POST-WAR BELGRADE IS CONTRASTED WITH THE NATURAL BEAUTY OF THE SERBIAN MOUNTAINS. THE NARRATIVE IS SUSTAINED BY SUSPENSE AND VIOLENT ACTION.

Kalemigdan Fort, Belgrade
'With the same unhurried air of concentration he did as he was told, working his way out of the gallery and turning to the left, across the expanse of gravel to the steps which led up into the old tower. The path led them across a sort of ravelin and through a gate towards the central bastion, and here he climbed the stairs slowly, pausing from time to time to take in the magnificent view which changed from room to room. A few couples sauntered in the sun on the terrace, and some children played about in one of the courtyards, but for the most part the fort seemed more or less deserted. He tucked himself in a corner of the battlements and stared out at the confluence of the two rivers which swirled away round the foot of the Kalemigdan. The Danube and the Sava met in a single jointless ripple beyond the Sava bridge and swept down, turbid and brown, towards the eastern flank of the city.'

The Main Square and Opera House, Belgrade
'They walked out into the main square of the town together and Methuen smelt the curious stale smell that the Yugoslav public seemed to carry everywhere with them: sour sunflower-oil and rancid "kaimak". It hurt him to see how shabby and frightened everyone looked. He had heard of police terror but this was the first time he had come across anything which permeated the very air of the town. The silence, too, was extraordinary; nobody sang or talked aloud, there were no shouts or whistling. Only the dull clump of boots on the broken and scarred pavements of the town. The scattered street lamps carved great pools of black shadow under the trees. At the door of the opera a crowd seethed, waiting to buy rejected tickets.'

Maglic Castle
'Yellowhammers and magpies frolicked in the trees, and here and there the stern rock-faces to their right stood back and fanned away into dome-like mountains, steeply clad with beech and fir, and showing small pockets of cultivation. A crumbling Frankish fortress dominated one height and Methuen caught the flicker of sunlight on something which might have been the barrel of a gun at the eastern corner.'

The Gorge of the River Ibar, near Kraljevo
'At the entrance of the sullen gorge, where the mountains rise to right and left, the road, railway and river, having conducted a seemingly endless flirtation, are suddenly squeezed together and pass through the narrow rock entrance side by side. Here the Ibar becomes swift, brown and turbid; giant poplars and willows, their roots gripping the shaly banks like knuckles, shade the whole length of the road. The air becomes dense with the smell of water, for several smaller rivers have cut their way through the mountain to empty themselves into the Ibar, and the crumbling rocky walls which flank the gorge are bursting with freshwater springs. The valley for all its gloom is alive with the ripple of bird-song which mingles with the thunder of the Ibar's waters as they roar down towards Rashka.'

Serbia - the Gorge of the River IBAR Paul HOGARTH '87

Serbia: the Studenica Monastery Paul HOGARTH 87

40

The Artist's Journal

Nothing seems to have changed since my last visit to Belgrade in 1967, some sixteen years after Durrell's posting as Press Attaché to the British Legation. An ambience of melancholy decay still remains the dominant feature of the city. A prime example is Trg Republike or Republic Square (Durrell's 'Main Square'). The sombre bulk of a closed National Theatre looms in the background flanked by modern glassy blocks and grimy classical façades. I try to enliven this forbidding cityscape by inserting an element of the theatre – a flamboyant equestrian statue of soldier-statesman Prince Miloš Obrenovič, liberator of the city from the Turks.

Although the scene of countless battles, Belgrade has little left of its turbulent past. The only ancient monument extant is the great Turkish fortress known as Kalemigdan, where Methuen meets Vida, a Serbian royalist. I haven't been at work for more than a half-hour when a uniformed custodian stands by my side and wags his forefinger. '*Nyet, Nyet, Nyet!*' he barks. '*Pospice, pospice* [permit],' he repeats. I show my passport and tell him I'm an '*Anglicani khudoshnik* [English artist]'. To no avail. Should I spend the rest of a precious day trying to obtain a permit? I decide to heave a forced sigh, pack up and find another vantage point where, concealed by bushes, I continue in peace. Moreover, my second version makes a much more interesting image.

Like Durrell, I have seen a great deal of Yugoslavia. While his duties took him into Bosnia, to Croatia, to Dalmatia, to Slovenia, to Macedonia and elsewhere in Serbia, my own travels (to provide illustrations for a *Fortune* feature on Tito's return to a free-market economy) had taken me more or less to the same places. But not to the hinterland of Serbia, which provided Durrell with the main locations for his book.

And so, eager to shake off the dust of Belgrade, I drive south on the *autoput* to the Serbian Mountains in search of the wildly picturesque Ibar Gorge and the medieval monastery of Studenitsa. Alas, my first night's stop at the Hotel Termal in the spa of Mataruska Banja, is a rude awakening to the realities of Balkan travel. The place turns out to be a Fifties monstrosity inhabited by battered elderly peasants who wander round like lost sheep in a Pinter melodrama. The next day, as an antidote, I depict Maglic, a starkly impressive fortress which dominates the densely forested banks of the Ibar. Some difficulty is experienced clambering down the precipitous slopes to put together a dramatic scene of the 'Ibar's waters as they roar towards Rashka' (actually they flow in the opposite direction towards Kraljevo). Finally I find a huge rock to perch on as the river's waters boil beneath my feet. Mindful of the vipers which Durrell states lurk between the rocks, I select a stout forked stick. I need not have bothered. There are no snakes, only teenagers, hundreds of them armed with pocket radios. They lurch down the rocky banks from a fleet of tour-buses like an invading army of goats, to relieve themselves in the Ibar's pristine waters.

One of the delights of travel is to stumble on the unexpected. Like the Cheddar Gorge, the Ibar Gorge has lost its primeval wildness. But a little further on, set amidst vast pine forests, I discover the King's Monastery of Studenitsa. A little worse for wear, but still enclosed within its original walls is this jewel of medieval Serbian architecture that moved Durrell to make it a prime location for his exciting story.

Studenitsa Monastery
'He crossed the first shoulder of mountain beyond the monastery and could not help stopping to admire the soft undulating mountain lawn through which his way led by a maze of paths, through fir plantations and groves of mulberry trees. The fresh smell of hay was delicious and in the middle distance he saw the higher slopes dark and feathery with beeches. It was quite hard to imagine that once he crossed the crest he would be far from towns and human habitations.'

BITTER LEMONS

Church of St Michael, Kyrenia
'Panos lived with his wife and two small sons in a house which must once have been part of the Church of St Michael the Archangel – up forty whitewashed steps, brilliant with sunshine, into a stone courtyard: the obvious site of the ancient acropolis of the town. The belfry of the church towered over us, its bell banging aggressively for every service, the lazy blue-and-white ensign of Greece softly treading the wind above the blue harbour.'

WHEN LAWRENCE DURRELL SETTLES IN CYPRUS IN 1953 HE ESTABLISHES A FAMILIAR PATTERN OF LIFE BUT THIS TIME HE BUYS HIS OWN HOUSE (A HILARIOUS UNDERTAKING) AND FINDS HIS CIRCLE OF FRIENDS AMONG THE VILLAGERS OF BELLAPAIX AND THE TOWNSMEN OF KYRENIA. HIS INTELLECTUAL FRIENDS DROP IN LIKE SWALLOWS. 'BUT THAT IS WHAT ISLANDS ARE FOR; THEY ARE PLACES WHERE DIFFERENT DESTINIES CAN MEET AND INTERSECT IN THE FULL ISOLATION OF TIME.' THE DEMANDS OF THE PRESENT REDUCE THE SPACE USUALLY DEVOTED TO THE PAST BUT THERE IS A PASSING REFERENCE TO THE KNIGHTS TEMPLAR WHO RESURFACE YEARS LATER IN **THE AVIGNON QUINTET**. THERE IS A SENSE OF TRANQUIL PERMANENCE: 'THE DAWNS AND THE SUNSETS IN CYPRUS ARE UNFORGETTABLE — BETTER EVEN THAN THOSE OF RHODES WHICH I ALWAYS BELIEVED WERE UNIQUE IN THEIR SLOW TIBERIAN MAGNIFI-CENCE.' THE TRANQUILLITY IS TO PROVE EPHEMERAL. THE TROUBLES OF ENOSIS, SO LIKE THOSE IN NORTHERN IRELAND, ARE TO DIVIDE THE HAPPY COMMUNITY INTO WARRING FACTIONS AND TO LOOSE 'THE EVIL GENIUS OF TERRORISM WHICH IS SUSPICION'. 'THE ISLAND . . . WAS SOON GOING TO PASS THROUGH THE EYE OF A NEEDLE — WITH NO KINGDOM OF HEAVEN WAITING FOR IT ON THE OTHER SIDE.' AS PRESS OFFICER, DURRELL EXPERIENCES THE TRAGEDY OF EOKA AT THE CENTRE IN NICOSIA AND LEAVES A FINAL IMPRESSION WHICH IS HAUNTINGLY ELEGIAC.

Kyrenia harbour
'When I was finding my bearings and conducting an initial exploration I lodged with my friend Panos, a school-master, in two small clean rooms overlooking the harbour of Kyrenia, the only port in Cyprus which – diminutive, cleanly coloured, beautiful – has some of the true Cycladean *allure*.'

Durrell's former house, Bellapaix
'The two floors of the house now began to represent themselves in their true colours as winter and summer floors. Below, a great fireplace, small kitchen, study and bedroom; above, the indescribable terrace which should later be shaded by its own vine; a large rambling old-fashioned studio room, a small hall with a fireplace, and an alcove set deep behind a pointed arch from the window of which my small daughter, if she sat up in bed, could gaze out at Turkey and see the fort of Kyrenia framed like a water-colour. Brick by brick, stone by stone, window by window, I watched it all put together by my friends with a sense of familiarity that one has sometimes when a poem "comes out" of its own accord like an equation, without having to be tortured or teased.'

The Tree of Idleness, Bellapaix
'The evening was very still, and the cool silence of the Tree of Idleness engulfed us like a mountain pool. Sabri was up there, sitting under the leaves contemplating a black coffee, waiting for me with particular information about carob-wood – he had saved me a special load. "Sit, my dear," he said gravely, and I sat beside him, soaking up the silence with its sheer blissful weight.'

BITTER LEMONS

In an island of bitter lemons
Where the moon's cool fevers burn
From the dark globes of the fruit,

And the dry grass underfoot
Tortures memory and revises
Habits half a lifetime dead

Better leave the rest unsaid,
Beauty, darkness, vehemence
Let the old sea-nurses keep

Their memorials of sleep
And the Greek sea's curly head
Keep its calms like tears unshed

Keep its calms like tears unshed.

Bellapaix Abbey
'I was prepared for something beautiful, and I already knew that the ruined monastery of Bellapaix was one of the loveliest Gothic survivals in the Levant, but I was not prepared for the breath-taking congruence of the little village which surrounded and cradled it against the side of the mountain.'

Salamis
'I busied myself in the little study, turning out a case of books. I found the old wicker basket which had accompanied me on all my journeys in Cyprus. It was full of fragments collected by my daughter, buried in a pocketful of sand which leaked slowly through the wicker mesh. I turned the whole thing out on to a sheet of newspaper, mentally recalling as I turned over the fragments in curious fingers where each had been acquired: Roman glass, blue and vitreous as the summer sea in deep places: handles of amphorae from Salamis with the hallmark thumb-printed in the soft clay . . .'

Castle of St Hilarion
'HL on St Hilarion, whose identity appears to be in some doubt. A pity, because the site demands a saint with a biography. He is, however, supposed to have retired to the castle and died there.'

Turkish and UN observation posts between Turkish and Greek Cyprus
'To Larnaca through an extraordinary landscape reminding one of Plato's God "geometrizing": low hills, almost perfect cones with levelled tops suggesting the Euclidean objects found in art studios. Wind erosion? But the panel of geometrical mounds seems hand-made. And the valleys tapestried with fat-tailed sheep, plots of verdure, and here and there a camel-train and palm-tree. A strange mixture of flavours, the Bible, Anatolia and Greece.'

LAWRENCE DURRELL'S COMMENT:
The two island stories anticipate and realize the violence which was to break out between the Greek and Turkish communities. In Rhodes it has remained latent, in Cyprus it erupted. Strangely enough, if Greeks in Rhodes failed to get satisfaction from a Greek judge they turned to the Turkish mullah to settle their dispute. In Cyprus there was no such accord. The monotheism of the Turks led to their intractability. On the other hand, the Greeks still had many characteristics derived from their ancient polytheism which should have made them more tolerant but they became intransigent 'to save face'.

Othello's Tower, Famagusta
'Treading the deserted and grass-grown turrets of Othello's tower one could gaze down at the ships unloading in deceptive peacefulness, or turn and remark along the shallow coastline the white scar of Salamis, whose bony ruins also testified to the inexorable pressures of time and history which every hero has thought to suspend by some finite perfect action.

49

Paul's Pillar, Paphos
'His words came back to me with redoubled force later that morning when I stood before the leaning black pillar against which Paul had been chained to receive the brutal thrashing which he no doubt endured with the soundless indomitable fever of his kind. It lies in a nettle-grown depression surrounded by dense greenery and buzzing with flies, a desolate and abandoned place – but then the whole of Paphos rings with desolation and decay; mean villages squatted out history among their fly-blown coffee-shops, deaf to the pulse of legend.'

District Court, Paphos
'All tragedy is founded in human comedy, and even here, at the turning-point in our affairs, the spirit of the irrational which always hovers over the Greek scene kept brushing us with its wings; it was impossible at Paphos, when the trial opened, not to be amused by the gallery of desperadoes who sat in the dock, so perfectly did they symbolize the ignorant and lovable peasantry of those islands where so many thousand Commonwealth troops were given shelter after the collapse of Greece.'

Former Information Office, Nicosia
'The Information Office had a beguiling air of good-natured shabbiness, and its awkward mirrored rooms gave one the impression of entering an abandoned barber's shop on the Rue Cherif Pacha in Cairo. I had been led to believe that much needed to be done, but I was unprepared to find so few of the means for doing it.'

The Gymnasium, Nicosia
'The Nicosia Gymnasium was a large rambling building inside the old Venetian walls; together with the Archbishop's palace it formed the spiritual nerve-centre of the Greek community. With its rococo-Doric portals it looked, as all Greek gymnasia do, like a loosely adapted design based on an early illustration of a Doric temple by Schliemann. But it was a handsome place with its broad roadway and feathery green pepper trees, and the little Church of St John opposite was a delightful example of Byzantine architecture.'

L D:
Archbishop Makarios was instrumental in getting Durrell appointed to teach in the girl's Gymnasium. He chose not to speak English but enjoyed correcting Durrell's Greek. No doubt, he foresaw that he was helping someone who would be sympathetic to Greek interests if, as seemed likely, he was eventually asked to work for the British government. At the time, Durrell was looking after Sappho, his four-year old daughter by Eve Cohen, single-handed and it was fortuitous that the Gymnasium was for girls – a ready-made crèche.

St John's Cathedral and old Archbishopric, Nicosia

Makarios Statue, Nicosia

The Artist's Journal

Above the harbour of Kyrenia or Girne, to give its Turkish name, the mountains loom as if out of a Hokusai print. Below, the horseshoe-shaped harbour is dominated by the largely Venetian castle. Once used by the British to incarcerate EOKA terrorists, it is now the headquarters of the Turkish Navy in occupied Cyprus. To my surprise, the local tourist office assure me that I'm at liberty to depict the picturesque scene. I manage to complete a view of the harbour when two Turkish marines appear to inform me it's *verboten*. I feign surprise at this and comply with assumed bewilderment, thanking my lucky stars the drawing was not confiscated.

Durrell was indeed right when he invoked Eastbourne and Folkestone to describe the ambience of the Dome Hotel. I am reminded of boyhood holidays with my parents as I gaze on the remnants of the once large British colony as they stride about in faded shorts and flowered dresses. Studiously, they keep apart from the tourists. And I don't blame them.

In nearby Bellapaix, or Bellapais, there's a sense of a paradise lost. There's a forlorn air about the village now deserted by its Greek Cypriot community. Less than a handful of Turkish Cypriot men drink under its celebrated 'tree of idleness'. The thirteenth-century Abbey remains in all its ruined glory, its Camelot-like appearance accentuated by immense cypresses, as does Durrell's beloved old Turkish house which he reluctantly left to live in Nicosia.

To the south, Famagusta, now Gazimagusa, remains hauntingly evocative of its historical past with much of the old city standing as if neglected, not ruined, unlike Salamis where the awesome spectacle of a once great city lies in ruins as far as the eye can see. As tourists wander about, even the more insensitive are visibly moved by a sense of tragedy. And there is more under the Mediterranean itself. Recent expeditions have discovered sunken ships and statuary, but recovery is unlikely until rival Greek and Turkish claims to what should be recovered are resolved.

As I drive from Larnaca to Nicosia another picture of a land divided dramatically presents itself. Near Dhali, the highway enters a lunar landscape of bleached white cone-shaped hills. On the highest are the observation towers of the Turkish Army with attendant United Nations Forces Truce observation posts. Facing both across a no-man's-land of minefields and barbed wire are the outposts of the Greek Army. Warning signs are illustrated with crudely painted skulls and crossbones, reminiscent of the figure in Edvard Munch's painting, *The Scream*. I find the scene a grim postscript to *Bitter Lemons* and with the help of binoculars depict it sheltered by a partially completed house.

Nicosia yields many locations unchanged by the passage of the years. I draw the classical entrance portico of the Pancyrian Gymnasium where Durrell briefly taught English when not writing *Justine*. And I only have to cross the street to depict the splendidly elegant Cathedral of St John flanked by the Archbishop's ornate old residence. A former Cypriot colleague identifies the building where Durrell worked as Public Information Officer to Sir Andrew Wright, the British High Commissioner. The Home-Counties-Bauhaus-style building is now the House of Representatives of the Cypriot Parliament. In Paphos also I find the former buildings of the British administration still in use. Sandwiched between the offices of the District Government and the Post Office is the District Courthouse, the same courthouse in which a group of EOKA terrorists were tried; and where Patrick Leigh Fermor, Philip Toynbee and Durrell sat together as observers.

There's a sadness, a melancholy about the colonies of the old Empire and Cyprus is of course, no exception. English remains the *lingua franca* and from it emanates the disillusionment which follows a struggle for independence, for it hasn't quite worked out like the idealists thought it would. I have almost finished my drawing of the courthouse when an elderly onlooker suddenly gives a cynical chuckle. I ask him what amuses him. He points to a banner hanging on one side of the entrance. 'We are asked to shed blood,' he adds, 'yesterday for the independence, now for the Mediterranean anaemia!'

The Bedestan, Nicosia
'I went down to the Turkish quarter and sat down among the carters and bus-drivers for a coffee and cognac in the very shadow of the Bedestan, the most haunting corner of Nicosia.'

THE ALEXANDRIA QUARTET

THE FIRST THREE NOVELS OF THE QUARTET ARE INTERTWINED, ONLY THE LAST IS SEQUENTIAL. DURRELL CALLS THEM 'A WORD CONTINUUM'. THE VIEWPOINT CONSTANTLY CHANGES AND WITH EACH CHANGE COMES A NEW REVELATION. 'IT WAS LIFE ITSELF THAT WAS A FICTION — WE WERE ALL SAYING IT IN OUR DIFFERENT WAYS, EACH UNDERSTANDING IT ACCORDING TO HIS NATURE AND GIFT.' AT THE CENTRE OF THE MYSTERY LIES ALEXANDRIA.

'An ancient city with all its cruelties intact, pitched upon a desert and a lake. Walking down the remembered grooves of streets which extended on every side, radiating out like the arms of a starfish from the axis of its founder's tomb. Footfalls echoing in the memory, forgotten scenes and conversations springing up at me from the walls, the café tables, the shuttered rooms with cracked and peeling ceilings. Alexandria, princess and whore. The royal city and the *anus mundi*. She would never change so long as the races continued to seethe here like must in a vat; so long as the streets and squares still gushed and spouted with the fermentation of these diverse passions and spites, rages and sudden calms. A fecund desert of human loves littered with the whitening bones of its exiles. Tall palms and minarets marrying in the sky. A hive of white mansions flanking those narrow and abandoned streets of mud which were racked all night by Arab music and the cries of girls who so easily disposed of their body's wearisome baggage (which galled them) and offered to the night the passionate kisses which money could not disflavour. The sadness and beatitude of this human conjunction which perpetuates itself to eternity, an endless cycle of rebirth and annihilation which alone could teach and reform by its destructive power. ("One makes love only to confirm one's loneliness" said Pursewarden, and at another time Justine added like a coda "A woman's best love letters are always written to the man she is betraying" as she turned an immemorial head on a high balcony, hanging above a lighted city where the leaves of the trees seemed painted by the electric signs, where the pigeons tumbled as if from shelves . . .) A great honeycomb of faces and gestures'.
(Clea)

JUSTINE

ALL THE CHARACTERS IN THE BOOK CONTRIBUTE TO BUILDING A MULTI-FACETED IMAGE OF THE EPONYMOUS HEROINE, WHO IS AS REAL AND YET AS MYSTERIOUS AS THE EXOTIC SETTING OF ALEXANDRIA, HER HOME TOWN. SHE IS PRESENTED PRIMARILY THROUGH THE EYES OF THE NARRATOR, ONE OF HER LOVERS AND FRIEND OF HER HUSBAND NESSIM, BUT THE PERSPECTIVE IS VARIED BY QUOTATIONS FROM LETTERS, DIARIES AND A NOVEL WRITTEN BY HER FIRST HUSBAND ARNAUTI. THE PANORAMA OF THE CITY AND ITS INHABITANTS IS ENIGMATIC AND SORDID, ROMANTIC AND GROTESQUE.

The Cecil Hotel

'I see her sitting alone by the sea, reading a newspaper and eating an apple; or in the vestibule of the Cecil Hotel, among the dusty palms, dressed in a sheath of silver drops, holding her magnificent fur at her back as a peasant holds his coat – her long forefinger hooked through the tag. Nessim has stopped at the door of the ballroom which is flooded with light and music. He has missed her. Under the palms, in a deep alcove, sit a couple of old men playing chess. Justine has stopped to watch them. She knows nothing of the game, but the aura of stillness and concentration which brims the alcove fascinates her. She stands there between the deaf players and the world of music for a long time, as if uncertain into which to plunge. Finally Nessim comes softly to take her arm and they stand together for a while, she watching the players, he watching her. At last she goes softly, reluctantly, circumspectly into the lighted world with a little sigh.'

LAWRENCE DURRELL'S COMMENT:
It is outwardly unchanged and was always preferable to Cairo's Shepheard's Hotel, now demolished, because of its proximity to the sea.

Pompey's Pillar
'The Cabal met at this time in what
resembled a disused curator's
wooden hut, built against the red
earth walls of an embankment, very
near to Pompey's Pillar. I suppose
the morbid sensitivity of the
Egyptian police to political meetings
dictated the choice of such a *venue*.'

LD:
A deserted area. When the moon is full it
seems so large and so close that it might
easily be swallowed. In high summer
Durrell used to take his friends there by
gharry after dinner or the theatre because of
the freshness of the sea breezes. He often
wondered who had put the Pillar upright
and how they had done it. The area is
thought to have been a Coptic cemetery but
the sphinx-like objects are probably Coptic
baking-ovens.

Lake Mareotis 'Premonitions of the dawn are already in the air as we cross the darkness of this lost world. Now the approaches to the empty water ahead are shivered by the faintest etching of islands, sprouts of beard, reeds and sedge. And on all sides now comes the rich plural chuckle of duck and the shrill pinched note of the gulls to the seaboard. Faraj grunts and turns the punt towards a nearby island. Reaching out upon the darkness my hands grasp the icy rim of the nearest barrel into which I laboriously climb. The butts consist merely of a couple of dry wood-slatted barrels tied together and festooned with tall reeds to make them invisible. The loader holds the punt steady while I disembarrass him of my gear. There is nothing to do now but to sit and wait for the dawn which is rising slowly somewhere, to be born from this black expressionless darkness.'

L D: A kind of Egyptian Camargue which is worth
comparing with the painting of the Camargue in *Quinx*. At one time it was even mooted
that bulls should be raised there for the Middle East.

BALTHAZAR

THE NARRATOR'S ROMANTIC ACCOUNT OF JUSTINE IS PUT UNDER THE MICROSCOPE BY DOCTOR BALTHAZAR WHO WRITES A COMMENTARY ON IT WHICH EXPLODES MANY MYTHS. THE NEW PERSPECTIVE IS MORE REALISTIC AND MORE ALARMING. THE POETRY OF PASSION HAS TO ACCOMMODATE MORE WORLDLY CONCERNS: THE EXTREMES OF TRAGEDY AND COMEDY ARE HEIGHTENED. DURRELL CALLS THE NOVEL 'INTERLINEAR', A READING BETWEEN THE LINES. IT IS A LAYERED NOVEL, A PALIMPSEST.

AT ALEXANDRIA

Wind among prisms all tonight again!
Alone again, awake again in the Sufi's house,
Cumbered by this unexpiring love,
Jammed like a cartridge in the breech
Leaving the bed with its dented pillow,
The married shoes alert upon the floor.

Is life more than the sum of its errors?
Tubs of clear flesh, egyptian women:
Favours, kohl, nigger's taste of seeds,
Pepper or lemon, breaking from one's teeth
Bifurcated as the groaning stalks of celery.

Much later comes the tapping on the panel.
The raven in the grounds:
At four thirty the smell of satin, leather:
Rain falling in the mirror above the mad
Jumbled pots of expensive scent and fard,
And the sense of some great impending scandal.

Great sphinx and pyramids, Giza

The Yacht Club
'But the great panels of the brass-framed windows in the Yacht Club blazed like diamonds, throwing a brilliant light upon the snowy tables with their food, setting fire to the glasses and jewellery and eyes in a last uneasy conflagration before the heavy curtains would be drawn and the faces which had gathered to greet Mountolive took on the warm pallors of candle-light.'

Statue of Mohammed Ali, Mohammed Ali Square
'It was already dark when I dismissed my taxi at Mohammed Ali Square and set out to walk to the sub-department of the Prefecture where Nimrod's office was. I was still dazed by the turn events had taken, and weighed down by the dispiriting possibilities they had raised in my mind – the warnings and threatenings of the last few months during which I had lived only for one person – Justine. I burned with impatience to see her again.'

The Grande Corniche
'Despite the season the seafront of
the city was gay with light – the
long sloping lines of the Grande
Corniche curving away to a low
horizon; a thousand lighted panels of
glass in which, like glorious tropical
fish, the inhabitants of the European
city sat at glittering tables stocked
with glasses of mastic, aniseed
or brandy.'

Pigeon house, Nile Delta
'The main gateway was flanked on each side by a pigeon-tower – those clumsy columns built of earthen pitchers pasted together anyhow with mud–cement: which are characteristic of country houses in Egypt and which supplied the choicest dish for the country squire's table.'

Nile Delta, fishing boats

The Tombs in Saqarra

'So, while I think of it, let me tell
you the story of Justine's laughter!
You will admit that you yourself
never heard it, not once, I mean in a
way that was not mordant, not
wounded. But Pursewarden did – at
the tombs in Saqarra! By moonlight,
two days after Sham el Nessim.
They were among a large party of
sightseers, a crowd under cover of
which they had managed to talk a
little, like the conspirators they were:
already at this time Pursewarden had
put an end to her private visitations
to his hotel-room. So it gave them a
forbidden pleasure, this exchange of
a few hoarded secret words; and at
last this evening they came by chance
to be alone, standing together in one
of those overbearing and
overwhelming mementoes to a
specialized sense of death:
the tombs.'

LAWRENCE DURRELL'S COMMENT:
It was a secretive place well suited for illicit
rendezvous.

MOUNTOLIVE

DARLEY, THE NARRATOR OF THE TWO PRECEDING NOVELS, APPEARS ONLY AS A MINOR CHARACTER IN THIS MORE TRADITIO-NAL NARRATIVE OF MOUNTOLIVE'S YOUNG LOVE FOR NESSIM'S MOTHER, A LOVE WHICH TURNS TO ASHES ON HIS RETURN TO EGYPT LATER IN LIFE AS BRITISH AMBASSADOR. PURSEWARDEN, A WRITER AND EMBASSY OFFICIAL, GAINS IN STATURE AND ACTS AS A CATALYST. THE SAME SCENE IS PORTRAYED IN ITS DIPLOMATIC AND POLITICAL CONTEXT; PRIVATE AFFAIRS HAVE UNFORESEEN PUBLIC REPERCUSSIONS. IT IS AN OVER-VIEW WHICH SHOWS THE DIFFERENT LEVELS ON WHICH PEOPLE LIVE.

MAREOTIS

Now everywhere Spring opens
Like an eyelid still unfocused,
Unsharpened in expression yet or depth,
But smiling and entire, stirring from sleep.

Birds begin, swindlers of the morning.
Flowers and the wild ways begin:
And the body's navigation in its love
Through wings, messages, telegrams
Loose and unbodied roam the world.

Only we are held here on the
Rationed love – a landscape like an eye,
Where the wind gnashes by Mareotis,
Stiffens the reeds and glistening salt,
And in the ancient roads the wind,
Not subtle, not confiding, touches once again
The melancholy elbow cheek and paper.

The British Ambassador's Residence,
Cairo

'Then at last the great car bore him smoothly away to the Residence on the banks of the Nile. Errol came with him to show him around and make the necessary introductions to the house-staff. The size and elegance of the building were exciting, and also rather intimidating. To have all these rooms at one's disposal was enough to deter any bachelor. "Still, for entertaining" he said almost sorrowfully "I suppose they are necessary." But the place echoed around him as he walked about the magnificent ball-room, across the conservatories, the terraces, peering out on the grassy lawns which went right down to the bank of the cocoa-coloured Nile water. Outside, goose-necked sprinklers whirled and hissed night and day, keeping the coarse emerald grass fresh with moisture.

He heard their sighing as he undressed and had a cold shower in the beautiful bathroom with its vitreous glass baubles; Errol was soon dismissed with an invitation to return after dinner and discuss plans and projects. "I'm tired" said Mountolive truthfully, "I want to have a quiet dinner alone. This heat – I should remember it; but I'd forgotten."'

The House of Memlik Pasha, Cairo
'Today in the sixties the house of Memlik Pasha has become famous in the remotest capitals of the world chiefly because of the distinctive architecture of the Banks which bear their founder's name; and indeed their style has all the curious marks of this mysterious man's taste – for they are all built to the same grotesque pattern, a sort of travesty of an Egyptian tomb, adapted by a pupil of Corbusier! Irresistibly one is forced to stop short and wonder at their grim façades, whether one is walking in Rome or Rio. The squat pillars suggest a mammoth stricken by sudden elephantiasis, the grotesque survival, or perhaps revival, of something inherently macabre – a sort of Ottoman-Egyptian–Gothic?'

The Nile river bank, Cairo
'She was staring unsmilingly at him. "I am nervous" she said at last with a little shiver. "Nessim, let us drive by the Nile for an hour and collect our thoughts before we go to bed." He was glad to indulge her, and for an hour the car nosed softly along the noble tree-lined roads of the Nile river bank under the jacarandas, its engine purring while they talked intermittently in low voices. "What worries me" she said, "is that you will have Memlik's hand upon your shoulder. How will you ever shake it off? If he has firm evidence against you, he will never relax his grip until you are squeezed dry."'

Sakkia in Nile Delta
'At the end of the long shady plantations, they encountered another, more familiar sound, in the soughing of the wooden water-wheels, the *sakkia* of Egypt, and Narouz cocked an appreciative ear to the wind. "Listen" he said, "listen to the *sakkias*. Do you know their story? At least, what the villagers say? Alexander the Great had asses' ears though only one person knew his secret. That was his barber who was a Greek. Difficult to keep a secret if you are Greek! So the barber to relieve his soul went out into the fields and told it to a *sakkia*; ever since the *sakkias* are crying sadly to each other 'Alexander has asses' ears.'"'

Caged-bird shop, Cairo

The Citadel, Cairo

LAWRENCE DURRELL'S COMMENT:
During the War it was out-of-bounds
and may well have been used by the
Egyptian police who play an important
role in the novel, but to have used the
dramatic image of the Citadel would
have given this element too great
an emphasis.

73

CLEA

THE WAR, IMMINENT IN OTHER NOVELS, HAS FINALLY BROKEN OUT. WHEN THE NARRATOR RETURNS TO ALEXANDRIA FROM HIS ISLAND RETREAT, IT IS TO FIND A FAMILIAR SCENE GREATLY CHANGED. THE FIRST THREE NOVELS WERE A RENDEZVOUS WITH ALEXANDRIA THROUGH MEMORY, THE LAST IS A REUNION IN THE PRESENT. THE REALITY SHATTERS MANY DREAMS, THE NARRATOR RESUMES HIS CENTRAL ROLE. 'WE WERE THREE WRITERS, I NOW SAW, CONFIDED TO A MYTHICAL CITY FROM WHICH WE WERE TO DRAW OUR NOURISHMENT, IN WHICH WE WERE TO CONFIRM OUR GIFTS. ARNAUTI, PURSEWARDEN, DARLEY — LIKE PAST, PRESENT AND FUTURE TENSE! AND IN MY OWN LIFE (THE STAUNCHLESS STREAM FLOWING FROM THE WOUNDED SIDE OF TIME!) THE THREE WOMEN WHO ALSO ARRANGED THEMSELVES AS IF TO REPRESENT THE MOODS OF THE GREAT VERB, LOVE: MELISSA, JUSTINE AND CLEA.'

The battlefield of El Alamein
'As the summer burned away into autumn, and autumn into winter once more we became slowly aware that the war which had invested the city had begun slowly to ebb, to flow gradually away along the coast-roads fringing the desert, releasing its hold upon us and our pleasures. For receding like a tide it left its strange coprolitic trophies along the beaches which we had once used, finding them always white and deserted under the flying gulls. War had denied them to us for a long time; but now, when we rediscovered them, we found them littered with pulped tanks and twisted guns, and the indiscriminate wreckage of temporary supply harbours abandoned by the engineers to rot and rust under the desert sun, to sink gradually into the shifting dunes. It gave one a curious melancholy reassurance to bathe there now – as if among the petrified lumber of a Neolithic age: tanks like the skeletons of dinosaurs, guns standing about like outmoded furniture.'

The Battlefield of El-Alamein   Paul HOGARTH '88

Café Pastroudi
'Mountolive, Amaril, Pombal and
Clea, two on each arm. We will
walk the whole length of Rue Fuad
thus and take a lengthy public coffee
on the pavement outside Pastroudi.'

LAWRENCE DURRELL COMMENTS:
It was much frequented by the women of
Alexandria because of its renowned cakes
and sorbets. It was also used by men
who wished to be undisturbed while
discussing important business.

Nile fisherman and family

The Arab quarter
'The whole quarter lay drowsing in
the umbrageous violet of
approaching nightfall. A sky of
palpitant "velours" which was cut
into by the stark flare of a thousand
electric light bulbs. It lay over
Tatwig Street, that night, like a
velvet rind. Only the lighted tips of
the minarets rose above it on their
slender invisible stalks – appeared
hanging suspended in the sky;
trembling slightly with the haze as if
about to expand their hoods like
cobras. Drifting idly down those
remembered streets once more I
drank in (forever: keepsakes of the
Arab town) the smell of crushed
chrysanthemums, ordure, scents,
strawberries, human sweat and
roasting pigeons.'

Fort Qait Bey
(built on ruins of the Pharos)
'We rolled past the site of the ancient Pharos whose shattered fragments still choke the shallows.'

L D:
It was particularly impressive in a sandstorm because it kept appearing and disappearing, now in focus now out, like a dissolve in the cinema.

The British Ambassador's summer residence
'"I think you know of me. As a friend of my brother (Pursewarden) I would like to talk to you." The invitation to dinner the following evening she described as "private, informal and unofficial" which suggested to me that Mountolive himself would be present. I felt the stirring of an unusual curiosity as I walked up the long drive with its very English hedges of box, and through the small coppice of pines which encircled the summer residence. It was an airless hot night – such as must presage the gathering of a *khamseen* somewhere in the desert which would later roll its dust clouds down the city's streets and squares like pillars of smoke. But as yet the night air was harsh and clear. I rang the bell twice without result, and was beginning to think that perhaps it might be out of order when I heard a soft swift step inside. The door opened and there stood Liza with an expression of triumphant eagerness on her blind face.'

79

The Artist's Journal

I arrive in Alexandria to recreate scenes for the novels of THE ALEXANDRIA QUARTET and *Constance*. From the balcony of my fourth-floor room at the Cecil I look out to a darkling blue Mediterranean ruffled by the prevailing north wind. Below, the Grande Corniche or Sharia 26 July, busy with morning traffic, stretches to infinity. In the distance the Corniche reaches Qait Bey, a Turkish fort built on the ruins of the Pharos lighthouse, once a wonder of the ancient world. In the other direction it sweeps on past the stunted statue of the nationalist statesman Saad Zaghoul to Chatby and Aboukir.

The Cecil itself was built in 1930 as a grand hotel. Vaguely Turkish Art Deco in style, its once spacious rooms have long been subdivided and the original furniture replaced with standard hotel issue. Several suites and rooms are named after celebrated Egyptian politicians but not one after the more distinguished *literati* who have stayed here. Although, to quote Durrell, 'stripped of all its finery and echoing like a barn with the seawind sweeping under the doors and through the windows' the place still possesses the indefinable style of a once grand establishment. I depict the Cecil with the affection I invariably reserve for such survivors.

Alexandria, Durrell claimed, could at one time, be compared very favourably with St Tropez. I can well believe him, after walkabouts in once fashionable quarters like Chatby and Rushdi. Nasser's revolution, however, ended that era and great Art Deco mansions and apartment buildings abandoned by their owners have been and continue to be demolished to make way for horrendously ugly high-rise blocks. I am therefore unable to find a candidate for Nessim's town house on Rue Fuad, now Sharia Horreya, or for his summer palace at Abousir. There are other casualties like the Fort of Kom-el-Dik and the brothel quarter.

There are however compensations as I get more closely acquainted with the city. In the once affluent and still leafy Mohammed Bey quarter I find Larry's tower workroom intact, perched atop the handsome turn-of-the-century villa still owned by Emilio Ambron, the Italian architect who rented the house to Durrell after his appointment as British Information Officer in 1941.

Further settings for *Justine* reveal themselves almost reluctantly. There's the Graeco-Roman Museum, Pompey's Pillar and the Hospital. But not all stimulate me to want to draw them. The classic sequence of the duck shoot on Lake Mareotis or Maryut, on the other hand, has been very much on my mind. I envisage a large water-colour. But when I finally arrive on the scene I view it with horror and incredulity. Once a paradise for wildfowl, fishermen and hunters alike, the famous lake presents a depressing picture: it is heavily polluted. That man can befoul his environment so mindlessly beggars description. Huge industrial plants line its shores, spewing toxic waste and raw sewage into once pristine, wind-whipped waters. Scattered colonies of ragged woebegone fishermen survive despite the fact that the few fish they catch and offer for sale are unfit for human consumption. Arrowheads of wildfowl fly overhead without stopping to the less sullied and more tranquil Lake Quaron which lies further south in the oasis of Al-Fayyoum.

BALTHAZAR

After miles of evil-smelling shanty towns and garbage-filled irrigation ditches, the royal pyramids of Saqarra suddenly appear like reproving phantoms from a less sullied era. My first stop, the Step Pyramid of Netjerykhet Djoser, provides a setting for the visit made by Pursewarden and Justine. The pyramid itself is a deeply impressive edifice, golden yellow deepening to warm sepia in the slowly dying rays of the afternoon sun. I eagerly depict its time-worn slopes. Not even a security patrol disturbs my thoughts.

The Pyramids of Giza with the attendant Great Sphinx are an even more impressive spectacle. As I think of all the artists who have depicted this celebrated scene – David Roberts, Edward Lear and William Holman Hunt to mention but three – I decide to make mine a comment. No longer do affluent Europeans and Americans outnumber all others. They have been (of course) joined by the ubiquitous Japanese. But most of all, by wealthy Saudis and their wives to whom a holiday in old Egypt is what old England is to Americans, or so my knowledgeable driver tells me.

A visit to Wadi-al-Fayyoum yields drawings of shepherds with their flocks of sheep and goats and wallowing water-buffalo. Pigeon-houses abound, Gaudi-esque structures, some as tall as three-storey houses. They are built of mud and wattle, with open-ended terra-cotta pots for the birds to enter. I am happily at work drawing one remarkable example when an animated entourage of shouting *fellaheen* make their appearance, led by an enraged farmer who demands £20 Egyptian (£5 sterling) immediately or my instant departure. I am willing to pay but my guide tells me not to, saying there are other pigeon-houses. Red with rage, the kulak farmer vociferously claps his hands to emphasize that I must be off his property. It transpires that my guide, eager as always to please, had already crossed the palm of an aged gate-keeper posted to keep away unwelcome visitors. But someone it seems, let the cat out of the bag.

Larry's eloquent description of the Yacht Club in Alexandria sets me off on another wild goose chase. I have a fantasy picture of the 'brass window-framed' Art Deco club-house, only to be informed that the building is now the officer's mess of the Egyptian Navy and naturally prohibited. At times like these, I curse all writers as Pied Pipers who incite the poor travelling artist, only to vanish into thin air with a hoarse chuckle. Miraculously, the

The house where Lawrence Durrell lived in Alexandria

Yacht Club survives as the Royal Yacht Club of Egypt and was even allowed to move its trophies and treasures to a new building (opposite Fort Qait Bey). So I do the next best thing, I draw the brass ship's bell and mahogany compass mounting of the *Afghanistan*, a survivor of the British invasion of Egypt to topple Colonel Arabi Pasha in 1881.

Alexandria locations for *Balthazar* are proving difficult to find. Most have disappeared. So occasionally one must make a mountain out of a molehill. One such subject is Mohammed Ali Square, now Midan el Tahrir or Liberation Square, I arrive to discover that every building of note has long since gone. According to Michael Haag's excellent notes for his edition of E. M. Forster's *Alexandria*, Durrell worked at the British Information Office nearby. The Victorian Cotton and Stock Exchanges were demolished in 1982. The French Gardens are now a bus and tram terminus. Unwilling to admit defeat, I draw the fine equestrian statute of Mohammed Ali himself by the French sculptor Henri Alfred Jacquemart. The same Mohammed Ali (1805–48) who gave away two of Alexandria's most precious monuments, namely, the two Cleopatra's Needles now in London and Washington, DC.

MOUNTOLIVE

Since my arrival in Egypt, I've kept an eye out for the edifices of Empire. My score hadn't been all that good in Cyprus. Now I learn that Shepheard's Hotel was burnt down in 1952 along with many other landmarks of British and foreign occupation. I'm delighted to learn that after all that turmoil, the British Ambassador's residence in Cairo – a prime location in *Mountolive* – still exists. And thereby hangs a tale. Demolition it seems was planned, especially after part of the ceiling of the vast drawing-room fell on the two Davids, Owen and Steele, at an ambassadorial function, much to the horror of the Egyptian foreign ministry who ironically regard the residency with nostalgic affection. It was Maggie Thatcher who came to the rescue. Following a state visit, she ordered complete restoration to former glory and hang the expense.

Built between 1890 and 1894 within the old palace grounds of Kasr-el-Doubara, it was the first new building in what was to become the European quarter of Cairo. Known as the Agency, the Residency and then the British Embassy, this handsome late Victorian building is now overlooked on all sides by towering apartment buildings. Its view of the Nile is impeded by the ever-busy Corniche. Ornate gates bear the monogram of Queen Victoria, while its palatial interior is redolent with the memorabilia of the old Empire. Portraits of proconsuls like Sir Evelyn Baring (Earl of Cromer) and Lord Kitchener jostle with water-colours of Upper Egypt by Edward Lear and imperial occasions by William Simpson, Special Artist of the *Illustrated London News*.

After drawing the Residency, I wander about the twisting streets of the Garden City to look for a likely candidate for the house of Memlik Pasha, Durrell's corrupt Minister for the Interior. The house is described as 'a sort of travesty of an Egyptian tomb, adapted by a pupil of Corbusier'. So it has to be Art Deco. The tree-lined streets of the Garden City turn almost in circles. In this once elegant enclave, foreign embassies and legations established themselves and continue to do so. The grand Levantine families however, have long since gone. Their stylish Art Deco mansions languish, divided into tawdry flats for the poor, their wildly overgrown gardens heaped with uncollected garbage and burnt-out vehicles. My first choice doesn't meet with the approval of the powers-that-be. I've almost completed the drawing when I'm ordered by armed guards to pack up and leave. It transpires that the house is the residence of an assistant government minister! I have better luck with my second choice, an even more stylish mansion on Sharia Ibrahim Pasha Negib.

The streets pulsate with an immense variety of popular life. Lines of men smoke *narguilehs* (hookahs). Pedlars offer you a sweet potato, an orange, a newspaper, or a glass of sweet tea. Caged bird shops are thronged with Saudi families buying singing birds or doves. Surprisingly, Cairenes seldom pause longer than a few seconds to see what I happen to be sketching. I soon learn not to show too much interest in mosques as this invariably creates a commotion. A *mullah* will suddenly appear to wave his hands about in a gesture that implies I'm *not* to do so.

CLEA

I spend a frustrating morning on the Grande Corniche of Alex between Chatby and Rushdi, looking for a possible 'Auberge Bleue', a location which occurs in both *Mountolive* and *Clea*. Durrell's description suggests a dinner-dance establishment with raffish overtones. I find a Thirties-style casino-*Palais de danse*-cum-restaurant and draw the place from across a crowded Corniche, only to be told a few days later by Ashraf Jacob of St Marks that the Auberge was in fact a hotel which was demolished in the early Eighties.

Better luck in the afternoon. I find the Café Pastroudi, the celebrated tea-room on the Sharia Horreya (in Durrell's Alexandria, Rue Fuad) where Nessim, Balthazar and Clea meet for an *arak*. The style is between Art Nouveau and Art Deco, probably inspired by the 1925 Paris Exhibition. The Café still retains the character of an exclusive club with its *carte* in French and Arabic. Turbaned Nubians in ankle-length robes flitter about dispensing refreshment. The clientèle is shabbily cosmopolitan. There's at least one Englishman, who looks like an undergraduate, savouring the ambience as he sips tea while reading a paperback which on closer inspection happens to be *Clea* – what else?

The former summer residence of the British Ambassador still dominates a pleasant park, the Sharia Mina, in the Rushdi quarter of the residential suburb of Ramleh. Built in the same handsome classical revival style as the Ambassadorial residence in Cairo with spacious Home-Counties-style gardens and a stable, the former Residency evokes the heyday of British influence. Here David Mountolive spent his summers in solitary splendour. Although no longer the Summer Residence (now the British Consulate), there's a spacious flat for the Ambassador and his family during the stifling summer heat of Cairo.

Another Alexandria subject, a street scene in the poor Karmouz quarter near Pompey's Pillar and the adjacent Moslem Cemetery, causes something of a mild sensation. But the need to attempt at least one large drawing of what Durrell described as 'the Arab quarter' gives me Dutch courage as this neighbourhood is certainly Arab. I well know that nothing interests people more than being drawn in the context of their daily lives. But I hope to get away with it. It has happened that a crowd will vanish before I'm even half-done. But not in this case. As I pencil in local characters who ply their various trades, I become instant street entertainment. There are roars of appreciative laughter and just as I'm about to make good my escape, a glass of tea is thrust into my hand.

In an especially eloquent passage, Durrell described the aftermath of the Desert War of World War II, following the Battle of El Alamein (23 October–5 November 1942; the scene of Montgomery's decisive defeat of the Afrika Korps which led to Rommel's final retreat and the subsequent collapse of the Axis Campaign in North Africa). I hope to emblematize the battle in some way. Almost obligingly, the twisted dinosaur-like wreckage of an Afrika Korps Troop Personnel carrier for the crew of an 88 mm field gun presented itself in the park of the Military Museum. Strangely, its violently buckled chassis makes drawing it all the easier. Once the terror of Eighth Army tank crews, it remains a potent symbol of those tragic days, set against a drearily despoiled desert landscape, enlivened only by the brilliantly turquoise Mediterranean.

THE REVOLT OF APHRODITE
TUNC

IO

In the museums you can find her,
Io, the contemporary street-walker all alive
In bronze and leather, spear in hand,
Her hair packed in some slender helm
Like a tall golden hive –
A fresco of a parody of arms.
Or else on vases rushing to overwhelm
Invaders of the olive or the attic farms:
Reviving warriors, helmets full of water,
Or kneeling to swarthy foreigners,
A hostage, someone's youngest daughter.
All the repulsion and the joy in one.

Well, all afternoon I've reflected on Athens,
The slim statue asleep over there,
Without unduly stressing the classical pallor
Or the emphatic disabused air
Street-girls have asleep; no,
All that will keep, all that will keep.
Soon we must be exiled to different corners
Of the sky; but the inward whiteness harms not
With dark keeping, harms not. Yet perhaps
I should sneak out and leave her here asleep?
Draw tight those arms like silver toils
The Parcae weave as their supreme award
And between deep drawn breaths release
The flying bolt of the unuttered word.

ALTHOUGH THE NARRATIVE FORM IS UNCOMPLICATED COMPARED TO THAT OF **THE ALEXANDRIA QUARTET**, THERE ARE INTENTIONAL ECHOES FROM THE EARLIER NOVELS: JULIAN AND JOCAS PEHLEVI RESEMBLE NESSIM AND NAROUZ HOSNANI, IOLANTHE AND BENEDICTA REFLECT MELISSA AND JUSTINE, THE UBIQUITOUS PURSEWARDEN GETS A MENTION BUT THE NARRATOR, FELIX CHARLOCK, IS A SCIENTIST, NOT A WRITER. THE QUESTION IS ASKED: WHAT IS THE RELATIONSHIP BETWEEN INVENTION AND CREATION? CONTEMPORARY CULTURE PERHAPS FAVOURS THE FORMER AT THE EXPENSE OF THE LATTER. CHARLOCK HANDS OVER HIS INVENTIONS TO AN INTERNATIONAL CONSORTIUM, MERLIN'S, WHICH PROSPERS WHILE ITS MEMBERS PAY WITH THEIR FREEDOM FOR POWER AND MATERIAL REWARDS. 'WE ARE IN THE SAME BOAT,' IOLANTHE SAYS TO CHARLOCK. 'BOTH RICH, CELEBRATED AND SICK.' THEY ARE NOT UNLIKE SCOTT FITZGERALD'S HEROES — THE CRACK-UP POSTPONED. BENEDICTA IS A SIREN WHO LURES CHARLOCK INTO THE STRANGLEHOLD OF MERLIN'S — 'THE SANCTITY OF CONTRACTUAL OBLIGATION'. HE COMES TO LOOK BACK ON HIS INDIGENT PAST WITH NOSTALGIA — 'AND FOR A FEW DAYS CARRIED ME BACK TO THOSE REMOTE UNHURRIED EPOCHS WHEN WE HAD BOTH TIME AND WILL TO DEVISE, TO EXECUTE.' IN AN ATTEMPT TO REGAIN THIS FREEDOM, BOTH HE AND CARADOC, A FALSTAFFIAN ARCHITECT, ARE DRIVEN TO FAKE THEIR DEATHS. ATHENS AND ISTANBUL INCAPSULATE THE OLD, HAPPIER WAY OF LIFE.

Plaka Taverna, Athens

The Acropolis

'The Parthenon left stranded up there like the last serviceable molar in some poor widow's gum. Ancient Grief, my Greece! "Art is the real science." Well, well. Where they made honey cakes in the shape of female pudenda. Yes, but the Acropolis then was our back garden – hardly a corner of it where we didn't make love. The smallness of its proportions gave it a monumental intimacy. In that clear hard enamel air the human voice carried so far that it was possible to call and wave to her from the top while she walked the Plaka streets below. "I-O- lanthe!"'

85

'The Blue Danube', towards Sunion
'As for the Blue Danube, it enjoyed
a mild repute among frequenters of
houses of ill fame. Its name, in
frosted bulbs, had been changed for
it by wind and weather; the letters
had either fallen out of their frames
or gone dead. All that remained for
the wayfarer to read against the
night sky now was the legend The
Nube, ancing, abaret. "I should like
to come" said I, and received a
friendly thump from the Cham. He
was delighted to receive support
from some quarter. His good
humour returned. "It is run by an
adorable personage, daughter of a
Russian Grand Duke, and sometime
wife to a British Vice-Consul, most
aptly so entitled, and she calls
herself Mrs Henniker."'

Naos, Hippolyta's country house in Attica
'Naos, the country house of Hippolyta in Attica, was large enough to suggest at first sight a small monastery skilfully sited within an oasis of green.
By contrast, that is, to the razed and bony hills which frame the Attic plain.
Here were luxuriant gardens rich with trees and shrubs within a quarter of a mile of the sea. Its secret was that it had been set down,
woven round a double spring – a rarity in these parched plains: oleander, cypress and palm stood in picturesque contrast to the violet-grey stubbled hills,
their fine soils long since eroded by weather and human negligence. The dangling rosegardens, the unplanned puffs of greenery
made full amends for what was, at close sight, a series of architectural afterthoughts, the stutterings of several generations.
Barns climbed into bed together, chapels had cemented themselves one to another in the manner of swallow-nests to unfinished features like half-built turrets.
One huge unfinished flying buttress poked out nature's eye, hanging in mid air.
One step through the door marked WC on the second floor and one could fall twenty feet into a fishpond below.'

87

The Golden Horn, Istanbul
'It must have been some sort of
festival day, too, for the sky was
alive with long-tailed kaleidoscopic
box-kites – and by the time we
reached the water under the Galata
Bridge to pick up the steam pinnace
which had been sent for me, I
could look back and upwards at a
skyline prepared as if for some mad
children's carnival. In such light,
and at such a time of day, the
darkness hides the squalor and
ugliness of the capital, leaving
exposed only the pencilled shapes of
its domes and walls against the
approaching night; and moreover if
one embarks on water at such an
hour one instantly experiences a lift
of the senses. The sea-damp
vanishes. God, how beautiful it is.
Light winds pucker the gold-green
water of Bosphorus; the gorgeous
melancholy of the Seraglio glows
like a rotting fish among its arbours
and severe groves. Edging away
from the land and turning in a slow
half-arc towards Bosphorus I
allowed Mr Sacrapant to point out
for me features like the seamark
known as Leander's tower, and a
skilfully sited belvedere in a palace
wall whence one of the late Sultans
enjoyed picking off his subjects with
a crossbow as they entered his field
of vision . . . The light was fading,
and one of the typical sunsets of
Stamboul was in full conflagration;
the city looked as if it were burning
up the night, using the approaching
darkness as fuel.'

Painted wooden houses, Istanbul
'But we were near in to the nether
shore now and travelling fast; stone
quays and villages of painted
wooden houses rolled up in scroll-
fashion and slipped away behind us.
Here, rising out of a dense greenery,
one caught glimpses of walled
gardens, profiles of kiosks
smothered in amazed passion
flowers, marble balconies, gardens
starred with lilies.

'Avalon', Merlin's house in Istanbul
'It was eerie as well as rather beautiful to pass in this fashion up the hill, guided only by the single cone of light which threw up silhouettes of buildings without substance or detail. Owls cried among the bushes, and in the heavy night air, the perfumes hung on, insisted. We crossed a ruined quadrangle of some sort, followed by a series of warrens which suggested kennels, ducked through an arch and walked along the side of a ruined turret on a broad flagged staircase. Now lights began and the bulk of the main house came into view. It suggested to me a huge Turkish khan built (as such caravanserais were) around a central courtyard with a central fountain; I heard, or seemed to hear, the champing of mules or camels and the whine of mastiffs. Up through a central massive door and along a corridor lighted with rather splendid frail gas-mantles. Jocas was sitting at a long oak table, half turned sideways towards the door which admitted me, staring into my eyes.'

LAWRENCE DURRELL'S COMMENT:
The place is invented, as is its name – which might have come from Ruskin translated by Proust.

Cemetery at Eyub, Istanbul
'Then again, with the same equivocal air – an expression of pride and sorrow almost – she led me through the beautiful cemetery at Eyub, among the marble incantations with their tell-tale-turbans and flower-knots. We came to one grave set in a small grilled enclosure of its own. I could not read the flowing Arabic inscription, of course, but below it, in small Roman letters, I saw the name Benedicta Merlin. There was no date. "Who is it – your mother?" I asked; but she only turned away abruptly, picking a stalk of green with which to tease her lips as she walked down the hill.'

L D:
Turkish graveyards recall the Crusader period, the transition from Byzantine to modern. They have a great tranquillity – people tend to lower their voices – but there is no suggestion of the sanctimonious. They are in no way melancholy but can provide a relaxing setting for eating and drinking and conversation as was the case in the cemetery of Murad Reis illustrated in *Reflections on a Marine Venus*. The suicide of Sacrapant from one of the minarets is all the more shocking. It is a warning, like the Capitoline geese, to the two lovers who witness it.

91

NUNQUAM

THE NOVEL FULFILS ARISTOTLE'S DICTUM THAT 'A PLAUSIBLE IMPOSSIBILITY IS ALWAYS PREFERABLE TO AN UNCONVINCING POSSIBILITY'. WHAT IS SO CONVINCINGLY SHOWN TO BE IMPOSSIBLE IS THE ATTEMPT TO INVENT A LIVING REPLICA OF A HUMAN BEING. THE BEAUTIFUL IOLANTHE CAN PERHAPS BE RECREATED IN A WORK OF ART BUT SHE CANNOT BE REINCARNATED BY SCIENTIFIC TECHNOLOGY. THE ATTEMPT TO IMPROVE ON NATURE'S ORIGINAL RESULTS IN A MONSTER WRAPPED IN AN ANGEL'S HIDE. HENCE THE REVOLT OF APHRODITE. THE LIVING DUMMY DESTROYS ITSELF AND THE GENIUS, JULIUS PEHLEVI, WHO CONCEIVES THIS ULTIMATE SCIENTIFIC OBSCENITY. THE NARRATOR, CHARLOCK, WHO INVENTS ITS MEMORY GIVES IT THE 'COUP DE GRÂCE' AND BY INHERITING THE FIRM OF MERLIN'S, A SYMBOL OF CONTEMPORARY CIVILIZATION, CAN OFFER ITS MEMBERS ONCE MORE 'THE FATALITY OF CHOICE' BY BURNING THE ARCHIVES OF THEIR CONTRACTUAL OBLIGATION. BEFORE HE CAN SURVIVE THIS FINAL TEST OF HIS HUMANITY HE HAS TO PASS THROUGH 'A DARK NIGHT OF THE SOUL' IN A SWISS CLINIC. MEMORIES OF ATHENS AND ISTANBUL, THE CENTRES OF AN OLDER CIVILIZATION, SEEM TO HOLD THE PROMISE OF A BETTER, MORE EXEMPLARY CULTURE. MODERN MAN HAS GONE ASTRAY.

PUNKS AT THE PARTHENON

Take me, now, I have never loved anyone
Or believed in anything,
And for some little time now
Have come to believe that I must be
A variety of mutinous angel of love,
Candent and absolute in my nothingness,
Goaded beyond reason by the phrase
'As above, so below' Confessions of Empedocles
Both high and low. (An ego poached in salt!)

Yet three of such kisses and you are hooked
As we say in heroin lingo,
And for gaff those stupendous thighs,
To lead you on and on, loving atrocities,
By sweet syringefuls to the land of sighs.

The Paulhaus, Lake Zurich
'Yet now that I am officially mad and locked away in the Paulhaus, it would be hard to imagine anywhere more salubrious (guide-book prose!) to spend a long quiet convalescence – here by this melancholy lake which mirrors mostly nothingness because the sky is so low and as toneless as tired fur. The rich meadows hereabouts are full of languid vipers. At eventide the hills resound to the full-breasted thwanking of cowbells. One can visualise the udders swinging in time along the line of march to the milking sheds where the rubber nipples with electricity degorge and ease the booming creatures. The steam rises in clouds. Billiard-rooms, a library, chapels for five denominations, a cinema, a small theatre, golf course – Nash is not wrong in describing it as a sort of country-club. The surgical wing, like the infirmaries, is separate, built at an angle of inclination, giving its back to us, looking out eastward. Operations one side, convalescence the other. Our illnesses are graded. A subterranean trolley system plus a dozen or so lifts of various sizes ensure swift and easy communication between the two domains. I am not really under restraint. I am joking; but I am under surveillance, or at least I feel I am. So far I have only been advised not to go to the cinema – doubtless there are good clinical reasons . . . There are many individual chalets, too, dotted about upon the steep hillsides, buried out of sight for the most part in dense groves of pine and fir. They are pretty enough when the snow falls and lies; but when not the eternal condensation of moisture forms a light rain or Scotch mist.'

LAWRENCE DURRELL'S COMMENT: It might be an illustration for a cautionary tale in *Struwwelpeter*. The minatory element in both novels is of their essence. The lake of Zurich in the background is a dead lake and has none of the beauty of Lake Geneva.

Ski-lift, Lake Zurich
'A few moments' waiting and then
all of a sudden the cabin gave a soft
tremor and began to slide forwards
and upwards into the air, more
slowly, more deliciously than any
glider; and the whole range of
snowy nether peaks sprang to
attention and stared gravely at us as
we ascended towards them, without
noise or fuss. Away below us slid
the earth with its villages and
tracery of roads and railways – a
diminishing perspective of toy-like
shapes, gradually becoming more
and more unreal as they receded
from view. The sense of aloneness
was inspiriting. Benedicta was
delighted and walked from corner to
corner of the cabin to exclaim and
point, now at the mountains, now
at the snowy villages and the dun
lakeside, or at other features she
thought she could recognise. The
The world seemed empty. Up and
up we soared until we had the
impression of grazing the white
faces of the mountains with the steel
cable of our floating cabin.'

L D:
Switzerland is more alive in winter than
in summer. When the snow melts the
lakeside becomes 'dun'.

Rue Toutes-Armes, Geneva old town
'Even old Geneva looked its best
with its snug Viennese flavoured
architecture and its melancholy lake
views; thawing ice was chinking
along the river where the dark
arterial thrust of the waters carved
their way towards the southern
issues – waters which would soon
see Arles and Avignon.'

L D:
The houses evoke a calm and stolid
bourgeois self-satisfaction; they reflect the
world of commerce and banking.
Manwick's Tea Rooms was invented.

94

Market of the secondhand booksellers, Istanbul
'Bookstores near the Mosque of Bayezid in the old Chartopratis or paper-market; here in an old Byzantine portico resided a turbaned and gowned old gentleman who sat at a table with reed pen and colour box, with gold leaf and burnisher, filling page after page of parchment with exquisite illuminated script.'

Grand Bazaar, Istanbul
'As for the Bazaar – despite its size he knew every flagstone, every stall; and despite gaps and changes brought by the times there was enough for him to evoke what was absent as we rambled about it. The circumference of the place cannot be less than a mile, while about five covered arcades radiate from its hub, the so-called Bezistan. It is really a walled and gated city within the city, and it claims to contain 7,777 shops. Mystic numbers? Vibart walked about it all with a sense of ownership, like a man showing one round his private picture gallery. He had, I think, come to realise how intensely happy those long years in Turkey had been for him, and indeed how formative, yet he had spent the whole time grumbling about books he could not write. The little square Bezistan, so clearly Byzantine in feel, is less than fifty yards long; square and squat, it spiders this stone cobweb. The one-headed Byzantine eagle over the Bookseller Gate places the building as tenth century, after which time the eagle became two-headed. The gates are called after the quarters which they serve, each characterised by a product – Goldsmiths, Embroidered Belt Makers, Shoemakers, Metal Chasers . . .'

The Artist's Journal

TUNC

I spend much of a fine autumn day leisurely drawing the Acropolis. Since my last stay in Athens – as long ago as the summer of 1952 – much has been done to restore and conserve this magnificent spectacle of the glory that was Greece. Exalted, I walk back to my hotel along the ancient path of the north side of the hill to the upper reaches of the Plaka. Much has changed here too, slums demolished to leave the best houses, and also to reveal the old Roman city, especially around the Tower of the Winds.

I find two more settings for *Tunc* in Sunion, a small seaside resort some fifty kilometres from Athens. The site is breathtakingly beautiful. In ancient times it was the port of Akri Sunio which faced the Aegean Sea at the entrance of the Saronic Gulf.

Incredibly, I find 'Naos' and the 'Blue Danube' without too much difficulty, or what I believe to be these houses. Nela Papaghymagis, Larry's Greek translator, informs me that 'Naos', Hippolyta's country house, was once owned by the Lindier family and was known locally as the Lindier House. But no one, young or old, knows of such a place. I make the obvious choice which fits Durrell's description in almost every detail. Unfortunately, the house faces the sea seated on a great cliff, and on both sides high walls conceal what Durrell described as 'a small monastery skilfully sited within an oasis of green'. After an abortive approach to the resident caretaker ('It would cost me my job'), I decide to draw it from the front at the safe distance of about fifty metres: the reason being that there's a very large Dobermann guard-dog which stands motionless, pale eyes glued to every movement I make, behind the cast-iron electronically controlled entrance gates. I work rapidly and think of the sacred dogs kept by Aesculapius in the ancient sanctuary of Epidaurus. But I very much doubt whether this dog would lick the sick. He would eat them. Not so far away, I discover a tumbledown *fin-de-siècle* single-storeyed villa undergoing restoration. Much to the astonishment of a stonemason and his apprentice, I complete the restoration as the 'Blue Danube'.

'Avalon', Merlin's house in Istanbul, on the other hand, gives me much more trouble. Durrell had based the house on one built by his friend, the architect Austen St Barbe Harrison. This was thought to be in Old Pera but I have a sneaking suspicion it could have been in Lapithos, Cyprus. 'You may well be right,' replies Larry, when I telephone him. However, the day ends with the discovery of a stand-in which appears in the shape of a battered fragment of a Byzantine fort facing the Bosphorus just by the Tophane Cesmesi fountain. The municipal authorities have made it into a public toilet, but I add certain significant elements such as old lamps and an ornate gate which I find in the nearby Kapatas quarter.

The shrine of Eyup or Eyüp on the Golden Horn outside Istanbul is said to be the holiest after Mecca and Jerusalem. Here Durrell set his scene of the lovers Felix Charlock and Benedicta, Merlin's daughter, discussing their fate as they stroll through the massed tombstones of departed Ottoman notables. The great minarets of the mosque (from one, Sacrapant commits suicide) add an eerie accent to this gloomily grandiloquent place.

NUNQUAM

Unexpectedly, a boat trip on Lake Zurich solves a problem. I take the excursion after several hours of driving about Zurich's suburbs, searching for a possible 'Paulhaus', the fictitious Swiss psychiatric clinic where the novel's hero Felix Charlock is imprisoned as a patient. I then spot among thickly wooded heights above the city, the château-like Grand Hôtel Dolder which looks an ideal choice. On closer inspection, the Dolder is indeed a perfect Paulhaus. I spend most of a morning delineating its magnificent alpine-gothic towers fringed by dense thickets of giant conifers set against the distant lake.

Several pages of *Nunquam* are devoted to Benedicta and Felix and their encounter with Julian on the Constaffel, the ski-slopes of the fictitious Paulhaus. But this location must be elsewhere as there are no ski-slopes in or around the city that are close to the mountains. I drive to Fiens on Lake Lucerne to look for an alternative location. Indeed, I might well have found the actual place where the maestro collected his material. At Pilatus the celebrated cable-car takes me up and above peak after mountain peak. At 1,415 metres or 4,643 feet I reach Fräkmuntegg, the second station of the *téléférique*. I clamber out to take my bearings and find a perfect substitute. The sense of solitude that Durrell described is overwhelming, disturbed only by the moving figure of a lone skier on a slope below. In the distance, the shimmering Alps give a celestial touch to the grandiose panorama of snow and ice.

Geneva has changed out of all recognition since Durrell lived there almost fifty years ago. Manwick's Tea Rooms, 'the headquarters of the Nannies of Geneva' although invented, was typical of the many English tea rooms which have long disappeared into limbo. Nonetheless, nanny-like expats are still to be seen taking tea in cafés like the little one which is to be found in the Parc Brunswick overlooking Lake Geneva. I therefore decide to go for a suitable image which conveys Geneva's 'Viennese-flavoured architecture'. I find an ideal subject, the Taverne de la Madeleine situated in the Rue Toutes-Armes at the foot of the massive Cathedral of St Peter.

A first look at the Grand Bazaar of Istanbul: the vast labyrinth of covered arcades, of workshops and retail outlets teems with shopping multitudes. Gates and streets are named after the many artisans, merchants and tradesmen who carry on their business here, as they have done for centuries. By the Beyazit Mosque, I find the Sahaflar Carsisi, the market of the secondhand booksellers, a picturesquely fascinating spot which attracts not only students from the nearby University but peasants from every part of Turkey and a horde of food pedlars.

As it gave me a slightly elevated vantage point from which to depict the animated scene, I had no alternative but to work from the entrance to a public toilet. Inevitably, a crowd gathers to watch me draw. When I object to one burly Turk, politely pointing out that he obstructs my line of vision, he replies in fluent colloquial English, 'What d'ye mean, I can't get in to have a piss because of your bloody admirers!'

SICILIAN CAROUSEL

THE 'CAROUSELLO SICILIANO' BELIES ITS ROMANTIC-SOUNDING NAME AND TURNS OUT TO BE A PROSAIC, ROUND-THE-ISLAND-IN-FOURTEEN-DAYS, PACKAGE TOUR. LAWRENCE DURRELL CASTS HIMSELF IN THE ROLE OF TOURIST WITH UPROARIOUS RESULTS. INSTEAD OF THE SELECT CIRCLE OF FRIENDS, HE CONDEMNS HIMSELF TO THE DREADED COMPANY OF TOTAL STRANGERS WHO RANGE FROM A PO-FACED ANGLICAN BISHOP TO A 'DEFROCKED' SCHOOL MASTER, THE DREADFUL BEDDOES, PESSIMIST AND MISANTHROPE. THEIR CHARACTERS UNFOLD WITH ALL THE SUBTLETY OF FICTION UNTIL THEY EVENTUALLY ACQUIRE A WARMTH AND HUMANITY AS THEIR WEAKNESSES ARE RELENT-LESSLY EXPOSED. THE FIRST IMPRESSIONS OF LANDSCAPE AND BUILDINGS ARE DEEPENED BY QUOTATIONS FROM THE LETTERS OF A DEAD FRIEND, MARTINE (THE MARIE OF BITTER LEMONS), WHO FINALLY CAME TO REST IN SICILY AT NAXOS. THEIR SHARED PAST IN CYPRUS ENCOURAGES COMPARISON BETWEEN THE TWO ISLANDS — SICILY, FOR ALL ITS GREEK HERITAGE, LACKS THE ESSENTIAL BOND WITH GREECE, THE LANGUAGE. DURRELL WRITES HIS OWN EPITAPH ON THE WHOLE EXPERIENCE: 'I REALIZED THEN THAT SICILY IS NOT JUST AN ISLAND, IT IS A SUB-CONTINENT WHOSE VARIEGATED HISTORY AND VARIETY OF LANDSCAPES SIMPLY OVERWHELM THE TRAVELLER WHO HAS NOT SET ASIDE AT LEAST THREE MONTHS TO DEAL WITH IT AND ITS OVERLAPPING CULTURES AND CIVILIZATIONS.'

LAWRENCE DURRELL'S COMMENT: The journey in the little red bus was too abrupt to allow sufficient time to warm to the environment and its brevity created a sense of panic, the need to get it written down before it vanished, and this in turn imposed a certain rigidity on the narrative. Although the other travellers were mainly fictitious some were drawn from life. There have been no complaints, so it may be assumed that the real characters have either not read the book or, if they have, have failed to recognize their portraits. Martine, the Marie of *Bitter Lemons*, is based on a former friend in Cyprus who married a Baron and died young. Her letters are invented but she is the Autumn Lady of the poem.

L D:
The style of Sicilian Greek temples is subtly different from that of Greece; it is imposing but also sinister. The proportions do not appear to be the same, perhaps because they are representative of the colonial. It is the kind of difference which exists between pure Gothic and its Victorian counterpart.

Temple of Concordia, Agrigento
'An ancient Athenian must have walked here with the sympathetic feeling of being back in Athens. And it was extraordinary to realize that this huge expanse of temples represented only a tiny fraction of what exists here in reality. The archaeologists have only scratched the surface of Agrigento; stretching away on every side, hidden in the soft deciduous chalk through which the twin rivers have carved their beds, there lie hidden necropolises, aqueducts, houses and temples and statues and all the wealth inside them of ceramics and jewellery and weapons. It seems so complete as it is, this long sparkling ridge with its tremendous exhibits.'

Temple of Zeus, Agrigento
'The great temple had, like so much else, been toppled by an earthquake; but the fragments had fallen more or less in order and some notion of its construction could be deciphered.'

Sicily: Temple of Concordia, Agrigento

Checking a Fusto, Azienda de Bartholi

Azienda de Bartholi, Marsala
'But the transition in time to a vast and cavernous warehouse in Marsala happened like a piece of *avant-garde* film-cutting. The jolt of stopping in the middle of a sort of impromptu cocktail party shocked us awake; for Mario had edged the whole bus into the echoing dark *cave* where, disposed along two vast trestle tables, was a constellation of beautiful bottles of every size and colour. We were to take part in a promotional *dégustation* for the famous product of the island.'

AUTUMN LADY: NAXOS

Under spiteful skies go sailing on and on,
All canvas soaking and all iron rusty,
Frail as a gnat, but peerless in her sadness,
My poor ship christened by an ocean blackness,
Locked into cloud or planet-sharing night.

The primacy of longing she established.
They called her Autumn Lady, with two wide
Aegean eyes beneath the given name,
Sea-stressed, complete, a living wife.

She'll sink at moorings like my life did once,
In a night of piercing squalls, go swaying down,
In an island without gulls, wells, walls,
In a time of need, all stations fading, fading.

She will lie there in the calm cathedrals
Of the blood's sleep, not speaking of love,
Or the last graphic journeys of the mind.
Let tides drum on those unawakened flanks
Whom all the soft analysis of sleep will find.

Bellini Monument, Catania

Ortygia, Syracuse
'The modern town has spread in a
smeary way towards the landward
side and the little island of Ortygia
is slowly becoming depopulated,
though for the moment it is full of
tumbledown houses of great charm
– like a little Italian hill-village sited
upon an ancient fortress. But the
presence of water, of the blue sea,
gave it radiance and poise.'

103

Art Nouveau gateway, Palermo

Palermo Cathedral
'Nevertheless when I actually stood in the hushed shadow of the cathedral in Monreale and waited my turn to enter its august portals, I knew what it was. It was as if we had turned a page in the story-book which was Sicilian history and emerged into a period which echoed the most unusual juxtaposition of styles imaginable. This pure Palermo Sicilian is an extraordinary thing, the most beautifully realized merging of the grave and lofty Norman shapes with riotous and intricate Byzantine and Moorish decorative motifs, a brilliant syncopation of the grave central theme.'

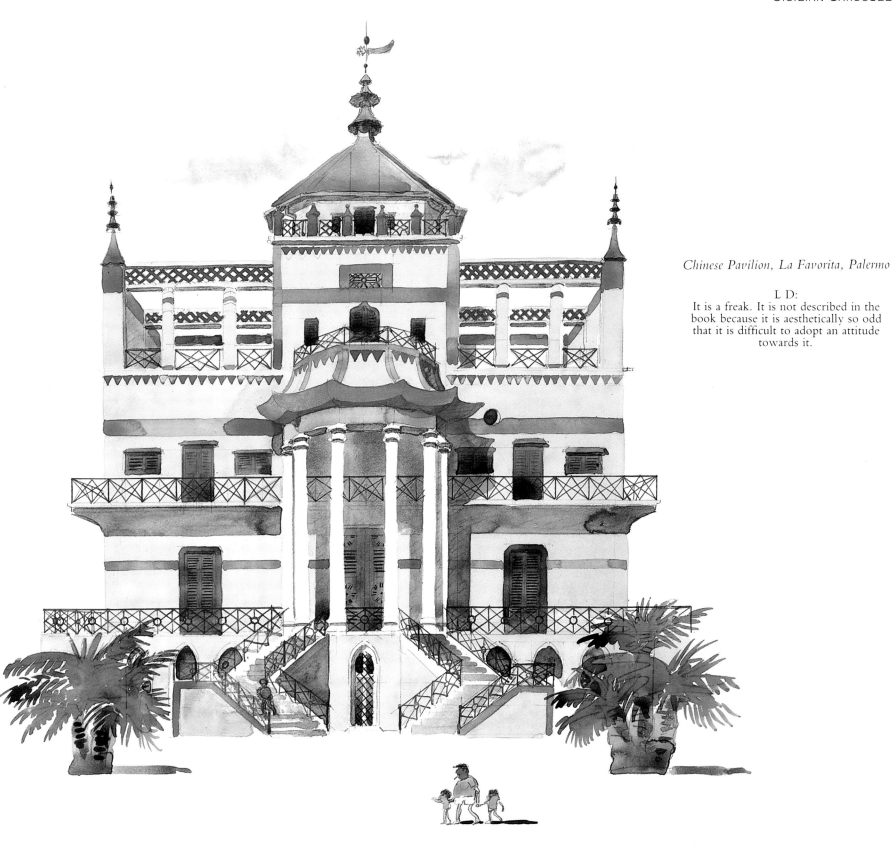

Chinese Pavilion, La Favorita, Palermo

L D:
It is a freak. It is not described in the
book because it is aesthetically so odd
that it is difficult to adopt an attitude
towards it.

Cefalû

'Indeed it was not long before one of the sharper loops of the coast road brought us up on a wooded knoll from which we saw the characteristic profile of Cefalû facing us across a blue bay. I found it astonishingly like the headland of Paleocastrizza in Corfu. It looked like a great whale basking in the blueness – a mythological ruminant of a fish, dreaming of some lost oceanic Eden, its eyes shut. The town clustered about it.'

Piazza IX Aprile, Taormina

'I left my bags and walked the length of the main street with its astonishing views. It was so good that it aroused indignation: one almost suspected it to be spurious; but no, it simply outstripped language, that was all. And a wonderful sense of intimacy and well-being suffused the whole place.'

Taormina

'It was the end of a whole epoch;
and appropriately enough I spent a
dawn in the most beautiful theatre
in the world – an act of which Etna
herself appeared to approve because
once, just to show me that the
world was rightside up, she spat out
a mouthful of hot coals, and then
dribbled a small string of blazing
diamonds down her chin.'

The Artist's Journal

Splendidly ornate buildings are more the rule than the exception in Sicily. I decide, however, that in Catania my subject should focus on the native son, namely the short-lived Vicenzo Bellini (1801–35) one of Italy's celebrated composers. After looking at the gloomy apartment in which he was born in the Piazza San Francisco, I choose the flamboyant monument to the composer in the Piazza Stesicoro. Guilio Monteverde's massive group has Bellini seated in his favourite chair, receiving the acclaim of the heroes and heroines of *Il Pirata, La Sonnambula, Norma* and *I Puritani.*

Ortygia is thought by Larry to be one of the possible places where Ulysses may have run into Circe. But I find no evidence to give shape or substance to the idea. Close by a medieval fortress built by Frederick II of Swabia, I have a notion and succumb to drawing a tiny square, the Piazza Largo della Gancia, perched on a massive segment of the ancient sea-wall whose very stones speak of countless invasions and foreign occupations. It may well be, that the rocks on which the wall was built were indeed those on which Circe sat to lure the unsuspecting Ulysses.

The guardian Temples of Agrigento appear like a line of heavy goods vehicles against the setting sun. Only the light of the following day reveals their tranquil beauty. I must avoid the distant view because to include them all would lessen the impact of my picture as each possesses a distinct *persona.* So I choose the Temple of Concordia. This magnificent edifice, seated on a flat escarpment, resembles a Grand Duchess of great age and refinement. Yellow ochre is the colour of her complexion, porous and pitted by centuries of sun, wind and rain.

Taormina is the island's most famous resort and is spectacularly impressive. Thankfully I'm here in December with hardly a soul about. After I draw the Piazza IX Aprile and the Teatro Graeco, I set out to look for the house where Frieda and D. H. Lawrence lived (1920–23). Eventually, I find it in the Via Fontana Vecchia surounded by surburban villas and holiday apartments. The Lawrences rented the house from an uncle of Signora Antonietta Falanga, who informs me that he told her that they argued each and every day. Unfortunately, she adds, her uncle was foolish enough to destroy the letters Lawrence wrote to him. The houses that writers rent reflect both life-style and what they can afford. No doubt found by the redoubtable Frieda, it boasted a big shady garden with an unimpeded view of the Mediterranean. Tall and ungainly, the house still retains the garden with its medlar, mulberry and almond trees. I imagine Lawrence looking out on the timeless vista of sea and sky and set the house against the morning sun.

Lawrence thought Palermo was 'where Europe finally ends. Beyond is Africa and Asia.' Certainly, its grimy streets, jammed with noisy traffic and uncollected garbage, remind me of Cairo and Istanbul. Blackened *palazzi* and crumbling stucco meet the eye at every turn. Street crime is rife. Young thugs, the *scippatori*, who work in pairs on scooters, prey on the unsuspecting tourist without mercy. Before you can count up to five, they're off with your wallet or bag. Yet the city is full of exotic corners: La Favorita Park being a prime example. Here, I found the Palazzina Cinese built in 1799 in Chinese style by Queen Maria Carolina as a retreat during the exile of her husband, Ferdinand I, the deposed King of Naples.

D. H. Lawrence's House, Taormina
'At dusk next day I walked up to have a look at the villa Lawrence occupied for three years. It was modest and quite fitting to the poems he wrote here in this pure high tower of silence which is Taormina at night.'

THE AVIGNON QUINTET

THE QUINTET ELABORATES AND EXTENDS THE FORM OF THE NOVEL EXPLORED IN **THE ALEXANDRIA QUARTET**. THIS CONNECTION IS ENHANCED BY CHARACTERS FROM THE QUARTET APPEARING BRIEFLY IN THEIR OFFICIAL CAPACITY OR BEING REFERRED TO BY NAME — A MONOGRAPH BY BLANFORD, FOR INSTANCE, RECEIVES 'A CONDESCENDING BUT FRIENDLY REVIEW BY PURSEWARDEN'. THE REJECTION OF CHRONOLOGY IS STRONG AS EVER — 'HISTORY WAS NOT PAST BUT WAS SOMETHING WHICH WAS ALWAYS JUST ABOUT TO HAPPEN. IT WAS THE PART OF REALITY THAT WAS *POISED*!' THE STRUCTURE OF THE QUINTET IS FOUNDED ON THE DEVICE OF HAVING A NOVEL (**MONSIEUR**) WITHIN A NOVEL SO THAT FICTIONAL REALITY BECOMES MANY LAYERED. A CENTRAL CHARACTER, BLANFORD THE NOVELIST, CREATES AN 'ALTER EGO' — SUTCLIFFE, ALSO A NOVELIST — AND THEIR DUALITY PERMITS A RUNNING COMMENTARY ON IDEAS AND EVENTS WHICH CAN BE BOTH PROVOCATIVE AND HILARIOUS. VARIATIONS ON THE THEME OF THE DANCE OF LOVE COME TO A CLIMAX IN THE FINAL BOOK WITH THE CONSUMMATION OF BLANFORD'S LOVE FOR CONSTANCE: 'WITH EVERY ORGASM YOU DROWN A LITTLE IN THE FUTURE, TASTE A LITTLE IMMORTALITY DESPITE YOURSELF. AND HERE I WAS HOPING NOT ONLY TO TELL THE TRUTH BUT ALSO TO FREE THE NOVEL A BIT FROM THE SHACKLES OF CAUSALITY WITH A NARRATIVE APPARENTLY DISLOCATED AND DISJOINTED YET INFORMED BY MUTUALLY CONTRADICTORY INSIGHTS — LOVE AT FIRST SIGHT, SO TO SPEAK, BETWEEN CONSTANCE AND MYSELF.' AT THE HEART OF THE QUINTET LIES AVIGNON, A CITY BOTH HOLY AND PROFANE.

LAWRENCE DURRELL'S COMMENT: The concept behind the Quintet is derived from the thinking of Einstein and Freud: the Five Power Principle, Unified Field Theory and Relativity of Einstein; impulse and inhibition from Freud. It is essentially what makes the Quintet a modern novel and separates it from the classical tradition. Sebastian's gnosticism might be described as Jungian, a philosophy of archetypes; it attempts to make the inexplicable too explicit and is the cause of his undoing. It lacks the totality of the psyche to be found in Buddhism. There is a circularity in the novels which is illustrated by the opening and closing images of Avignon. The novels are, in a sense, stereophonic and stereoscopic. All the characters are aspects of *one* character, Constance, and if they could be realized in 'the reality prime' of Blanford's final statement in *Quinx*, they would be fused into an ideal concept. Another way of looking at the novels is to compare them to the cluster of lenses seen in the magnification of a fly's eye; the more it is enlarged, the more complex it becomes.

'But we had lost time, we had lost quite a bit of time, and it was late evening before we suddenly rounded a curve of the great river and were treated to a spectacle made more remarkable by a suddenly visible moon rising in rhetorical splendour over the ramparts of Avignon. High above the city perched the Rocher des Doms – the hanging gardens of this deserted Babylon. It was as if fate had chosen to delay us in order to repay us with its inspiring entry into the city which was later to come to mean so much to us – we did not know any of this then. Now, as I think back, I try to disinter that first impression – the marvellous silhouette of the town magnetically lit by moonlight pouring over it from the direction of the Alpilles. It is still the best way to see it – by water and from afar, and with the historic broken bridge pointing its finger across the river. And the little shrine to Saint Nicholas with its bright lamps of benediction for seafaring folk. We had been gliding for nearly an hour among silent islands and deserted channels, watching the bare spars of the Cevennes rise on the night sky. And now suddenly this severe magic. It took much more experience of the town to come to the astonishing conclusion that it was only beautiful in profile – the actual Palaces of the Popes are hideous packing-cases of an uncouth ugliness. Nothing here was built for charm or beauty – everything was sacrificed to the safety of the treasures which these buildings housed. But you must walk about the town to find this out. It is a cathedral to Mammon. It was here our Judeo-Christian culture finally wiped out the rich paganism of the Mediterranean! Here the great god Pan was sent to the gas-chambers of the Popes. Yet seen from a long way off the profile and the promise of the town – they are heartbreaking in their sweetness of line; and by the light of the moon marmoreal in their splendour.' (Livia)

Avignon from Ile de la Barthelasse

MONSIEUR

THE EXPOSITION IN THIS NOVEL IS EVEN MORE COMPLEX THAN IN THE ALEXANDRIA QUARTET. IT IS NOT SO MUCH EVENTS THAT ARE REVIEWED AS THE FICTIONAL REALITY OF THE CHARACTERS. IN AN ENVOI, DURRELL SUMMARIZES THE LITERARY MAZE BY SHOWING THAT BLANFORD HAS ASSUMED DURRELL'S PERSONA AS THE AUTHOR OF MONSIEUR, AND CREATED THE FICTITIOUS NOVELIST SUTCLIFFE WHO INVEIGHS AGAINST A POPULAR NOVELIST, BLOSHFORD, WHO IS IN FACT/FICTION, BLANFORD. IT IS A KALEIDOSCOPE OF MASKS. 'HOW REAL IS REALITY?' THE INVOLVED LITERARY FRAMEWORK IS REFLECTED IN THE CENTRAL 'HAPPY TRINITY OF LOVERS': PIERS DE NOGARET, THE SEIGNEUR OF VERFEUILLE, HIS SISTER SYLVIE AND HER HUSBAND, BRUCE DREXEL. THEY ATTRACT INTO THEIR CLOSED CIRCLE FOUR DISPARATE CHARACTERS: AKKAD, PIERS' EGYPTIAN GNOSTIC GURU; SUTCLIFFE, A NOVELIST MARRIED TO BRUCE'S SISTER PIA; HIS FRIEND TOBY, AN OXFORD DON; AND SABINE, A WANDERING JEWESS. AS IN THE QUARTET, NOTEBOOKS, DIARIES, LETTERS, APHORISMS, FRAGMENTS OF AUTOBIOGRAPHY AND SUTCLIFFE'S 'ROMAN À CLEF' EXTEND THE VIEWPOINT OF THE NARRATOR, BRUCE DREXEL. THE ELABORATE RITUAL OF THE STRUCTURE IS COMPLEMENTED BY THE EXOTIC SETTINGS.

The Nilometer, Cairo
'It was not long before we had passed the points of the Nilometer – and then the broad hauntingly beautiful river opened its reaches to us like arms and we found ourselves gliding across a floor of dark glass which the evening light was turning to gold.'

LAWRENCE DURRELL'S COMMENT:
Durrell used to ride out to it on horseback to take a swim in the Nile.

The station, Avignon
'And so at long last to reach home, to clatter softly and wearily into the empty station – that historic point of return and departure: but this time alone. It has always afflicted me with a profound love-dread, this shabby little station, because so often when I returned Sylvie was waiting for me on the platform, hand in hand with her nurse, distractedly gazing about her. I was always looking out for her, I suppose. The train sighs to a halt and the rasping announcements begin in the accents of the Midi. I stand paralysed among the lighted windows gazing about me. It never changes; it looks so homely, so provisional, so grubby-provincial. You could never deduce from it the existence of the cruel and famous town to which it belongs.'

The Palais des Papes, Avignon
'My slow footsteps crunched on the gravel. Below loomed the sinfully ugly palaces of the Popes in all their blockish magnificence, overshadowing the town which despite the resonance of its name was still hardly more than an overgrown village.'

L D:
It is Christianity's graveyard.
The fortified honesty of Fort
St André, illustrated in *Constance*,
is in stark contrast.

The château of Verfeuille in the Alpilles

'It stands high up on the westward slopes of the Alpilles and from the highest orchards you can see not only misty Avignon in the plains below, but snatches of Arles and Tarascon as well. The winding roads lead steadily upwards towards it with a graceful inevitability, passing through rich olive holdings, the grey-silver leaves ashiver at the least caress of the mistral. The plots around the old house are so rich in springs, and the soil so correspondingly rich and loamy, that the ancients planted oak and plane and chestnut to make a verdant green shade around the house and protect it from sun and wind alike. Colonies of nightingales sing there by day and night to the tune of splashing water, while the hum of the cicada, deafening in August, provided a steady drizzle, as if of strings, as a background. Of the twin lions guarding the gates of the lodge one had lost a paw and the other half of the ceremonial sword he once held so proudly, point downward; as for the massive wrought-iron gates themselves, they had been carried away and melted down as a contribution to the war effort of fourteen-eighteen. The weeds have long since turned the gravel driveway to a mossy causeway where the wheels of a car tend to skid slightly in wet weather.

114

On this unexpected carpet of silence
one turns and twines for what seems
an age before the house comes into
view, perched slightly at an angle in
order to take the best of the sun
aspects and set a stout shoulder to
the northern quarter from where the
butting mistral blows. The
windows, so tall and narrow, wear
deep stone eyebrows, while the high
donjon, a prodigiously strong
square tower, dating from the
twelfth century, centres the whole
mass, giving a minatory touch of
fortress to what is now a
comfortable dwelling merging into a
farmhouse with all its clumsy
dependencies – barns and stables,
wine-magazines and olive presses.
The noise of cattle and poultry rules
here, and the prismatic dust hangs
in sunbeams. None of this will ever
change. The whole of this heavy
mass with its grilled windows
encloses the grand central courtyard
to which one gains access via a
deeply vaulted passage-way – an
easily defensible feature; this in turn
leads to the vital heart of the place,
the great well-head with its carved
crucifix and its benches. At each
corner of the court rises a quaint
and crusty little *tourelle* from which
the besieged could keep up a raking
fire along the thick walls.'

L D:
Much of its character derives from its
setting.

The Grand Canal, Venice
'Blanford re-read these words with a pang which translated itself into an actual touch of angina as he sat in his bath chair, high over the lagoons, and let his melancholy eyes wander along the delectable contours of dying Venice – the orchestra of divine buildings hallowed by the opalescent water-dusk.'

L D: Venice is not unlike Avignon, which seems to rise out of the waters of the Rhône. Both are decadent.

117

LIVIA

THE NOVEL PRESENTS THE 'REAL REALITY' OF BLANFORD'S SEMINAL EXPERIENCES IN AVIGNON ON THE EVE OF THE WAR. THE EVENTS IN **MONSIEUR** CAN BE SEEN AS THE FICTIONAL PROJECTION OF THESE EXPERIENCES. THE TWO NOVELS ARE PARALLEL AND INTERWOVEN. BLANFORD COMMUNES WITH HIS CREATION AND 'ALTER EGO' SUTCLIFFE ON THEIR MUTUAL INVOLVEMENT: BOTH ARE NOVELISTS; THEIR WIVES, LIVIA AND PIA, ARE LESBIANS; THEY KNOW TWO BANKERS, LORDS GALEN AND BANQUO, WHO HAVE ERRANT DAUGHTERS; EACH MARRIES INTO AN INTIMATE TRIANGLE — BLANFORD INTO THE CLOSE FAMILY OF CONSTANCE, LIVIA AND THEIR BROTHER HILARY AT THE CHÂTEAU OF TU DUC; SUTCLIFFE THROUGH BRUCE'S SISTER INTO THE 'HAPPY TRINITY OF LOVERS' AT THE CHÂTEAU OF VERFEUILLE. CHARACTERS FROM **MONSIEUR** ALSO APPEAR 'IN PROPRIA PERSONA' IN **LIVIA**. THE MESHING IS INTRICATE AND TAUT. AVIGNON IS STILL OMNI-PRESENT, THE LURE OF PROVENCE AS STRONG, BUT THE TIME HAS CHANGED — THE IDYLL IS ON THE BRINK OF DISSOLUTION WITH THE ONSET OF WAR; WHAT IS RECALLED AS THE PAST IN **MONSIEUR** IS THE INTRACTABLE PRESENT IN **LIVIA**.

Fontaine-de-Vaucluse

'Often, looking back on this halcyon period, Blanford had the sudden vision of them all, standing upon the iron bridge at the Fountain of Vaucluse, gazing down into the trout-curdled water and listening to the roar of the spring as it burst from the mountain's throat and swept down past them, thick with loitering fish.'

The Château of Tu Duc, Tubain, southern Vaucluse

'But recently, with the death of an old aunt, young Constance had inherited the little château of Tu Duc in the southern Vaucluse, not far from Avignon. The Duchess of Tu, then, was the obvious nickname for her. The children had spent many holidays there once upon a time in their extreme youth; but in her old age the aunt became first eccentric, and then mentally unstable; she turned recluse, locked herself up, and allowed the whole place to fall into ruins around her. The rain and the wind settled down to finish what negligence had begun; the weight of winter snow cracked the black tiles of the roofs and entered the rooms, with their strange scrolled bull's-eye windows. In the rambling, disorderly park, old trees had fallen everywhere, blocking the paths, crushing the summer-house under their weight.

118

Rue des Teinturiers
'He moved towards the little Chapel of
the Grey Penitents set incongruously
upon its dark canal with the stout
wooden waterwheels forever turning
with their slopping and swishing
sound.'

LAWRENCE DURRELL'S COMMENT:
Despite the waterwheels, it is a sinister
quarter of Avignon. There had been a
massacre of heretics there under the
Inquisition.

The Chapel of the Grey Penitents, Avignon

120

*The Auberge des Aubergines,
Pont du Gard*

'The auberge was a strange, rambling
old place, admirably suited to this kind
of initiative, with its collection of Swiss
chalets hugging the cliffs of the
Gardon, buried in plane-shade, leaning
practically over the green water.
Though it was not a residential hotel it
had a series of large inter-connecting
upper rooms which in summer
managed to accommodate tourist
groups or clubs devoted to
archaeology or Roman history who
selected the monument as a point of
rendezvous, and sometimes camped
out in the neighbouring green glades
along the river. The cuisine was what
had made it famous, and this was, of
course, an important part of the spree.
But it was not all, for the Prince, who
was a man of the world, knew his
France well. He knew that in this
spirited Republic any citizen may call
upon the *préfet* of any region to
floodlight a notable monument at a
purely nominal cost, simply to grace
his dinner. When he himself had been
young and madly in love with his
Princess Fawzia he had offered her
dinner here, served on the bridge itself
by his liveried waiters; just the two of
them, quite alone. He always
remembered this early part of his
married life with emotion. And now
the great golden span of the Roman
aqueduct was going to hover above
their revels, its honey-gold arches
fading into the velvet sky of Provence.
His heart leaped in his breast when he
thought of it. He became absolutely
concave with joy. No detail must be
left to chance.'

121

CONSTANCE

SOME OF THE CHARACTERS IN LIVIA REMAIN IN OR RETURN TO AVIGNON TO SUFFER THE BRUTALITY OF THE NAZI 'OCCUPATION', OTHERS ARE DISPERSED TO THE WAR-TIME LIMBOS OF EGYPT AND GENEVA WHERE THEIR LIVES INTERACT IN NEW DISPOSITIONS AND COMMINGLE WITH CHARACTERS FROM MONSIEUR, WHO SOMETIMES APPEAR AS THEMSELVES, SOMETIMES IN DISGUISE. IT IS A PROCESS OF LITERARY RESURRECTION AND TRANSMOGRI- FICATION EPITOMIZED BY BLANFORD AND SUTCLIFFE, THE NOVELISTS, WITH CONSTANCE ACTING AS INTERMEDIARY. BLAN- FORD SAYS, 'I INVENTED A MAN I CALLED SUTCLIFFE — FOR LACK OF ANYTHING BETTER — AND HE BECAME ALTOGETHER TOO REAL.' CONSTANCE ECHOES HIS STATEMENT, 'BY THE WAY, I THOUGHT FOR A LONG TIME YOUR SUTCLIFFE WAS IMAGINARY, BUT I FIND HE IS ALL TOO REAL.' SHE CONFRONTS SUTCLIFFE HIMSELF WITH HER DISCOVERY, 'SO AFTER ALL YOU ARE REAL,' TO WHICH HE REPLIES, 'EVERYBODY IS REAL.' THE AMBIGUITY IS HEIGHT- ENED RATHER THAN EXPOSED WHEN BLANFORD AND SUTCLIFFE MEET FACE TO FACE IN A SWISS CLINIC. THERE IS NO AMBIGUITY IN THE DAY OF LIBERATION FOR AVIGNON.

LAWRENCE DURRELL'S COMMENT: The trinities of lovers are all part of the essence of Constance in whom they are fused. The structure of the Quintet is very carefully conceived because it has to be strong enough to carry 'the voltage' of the ideas – like an electric cable conducting the massive force of electricity.

Coptic monastery of Aby Fahym
in the desert

'We came at last to a small oasis and a series of grey escarpments, forms of striated rock, which shouldered up into the sky. "Look!" someone cried as we rounded a shoulder of dune. We saw a small oasis and within a few hundred yards the Coptic monastery came into view. Aby Fahym must once have been very beautiful, though now it was rather knocked about; one had to decipher its turrets and crocketed belfries anew to rediscover its original shape and style. But almost any building in that strange, romantic site would have seemed compelling to the imagination. The two main granaries were joined by a high ramp in the form of a bridge. The Prince was highly delighted and gazed at the old place through his glasses, exclaiming, "Well, it's still there, the old Bridge of Sighs. They haven't knocked it down after all."'

L D:
The monastery was invented. The romantic image of the Bridge of Sighs was introduced so that it could be shattered by the reality of the shells which killed Sam and critically wounded Blanford. The incident was not preconceived but came into the mind fully-fledged.

The Bar de la Navigation, Geneva
'The street in Geneva at the end of which the old Bar de la Navigation stands runs back from the lakeside with its bulky Corniche and scrambles up a steepish slope. It is an undecided sort of street, it seems at cross-purposes with itself, for it begins as a modest side-street, becomes for a block or so a wider boulevard, then breaks off abruptly to become a narrow dog-leg passage giving on to an evil-smelling court full of lidless dustbins. It was precisely this air of lugubrious secrecy that endeared itself to our hero (heroes, rather, for Toby had appeared in Geneva to join forces with Sutcliffe). It seemed to them the ideal place for those confidential mid-morning potations and games of pool for which the Foreign Office had invented the phrase "elevenses", after the hour of the morning when one feels one most needs a short swift drink, or a long "unwinder", to use slang.'

L D:
It was a meeting place not unlike the Café Pastroudi illustrated in *Clea.* At the time, the rooms above it were boarded up.

The Palace of Montaza, Alexandria
'We went ashore in darkness in a large
motor launch belonging to the
Egyptian navy and landed at the water-
gate of a palace plunged in utter
darkness; then, after much chaffering,
somewhere a switch was thrown and a
sort of combination of Taj Mahal and
Eiffel Tower blared out upon the
night. It was my first exposure to
Egyptian Baroque, so the simile is
surprisingly apt. To blare, to bray – so
much light in so many mirrors of so
many colours – the effect was
polymorphous perverse, so to
speak . . . I realized that I was going to
fall in love with the place – I saw that it
was a huge temple of inconsequences.'

CAFÉ DOLE: AVIGNON

Come sit with me in a dead café:
A puff of cognac or a sip of smoke,
And pray for some prolific light
To warm up a dead man's hope.

The veteran with no arm can press
The phantom in his sleeve,
The aching stump insists
And nothing can relieve.

Late cats, the city's thumbscrews, twist.
Night falls in its profuse derision,
Gives candle-power to others' lives
When the absent are so much missed,
Yet cancels in us the primal vision.

Come random with me in the rain
In ghostly harness like a dream
Down streets and squares of saddened dark
Where nothing moves that does not seem.

The Europa Hotel, Avignon
'The Prince rubbed his hands with anticipation – he was looking forward to a hot bath and a drink. But the old Europa looked hopelessly unkempt. Its pleasant inner patio was adrift with unswept leaves. Its dim and makeshift lighting arrangements argued a power shortage. Moreover it was unheated; the main lounge was cold and damp. The manager came to greet them – he knew them of old, but it was with sadness that he advanced to take the hands of the Prince. "Excellency," he said sadly, and made a vague gesture which somehow expressed all the unhappy circumstances with which they would have to come to terms in this new world.'

L D:
It is the finest, not the grandest, hotel in Europe. On the occasions when Durrell travelled between Greece and England by car before the War, he always tried to find the money from somewhere to stay there. After the ravages of war it has returned to its former glory. It is a real monument to the past – like the Acropolis.

The old church, Montfavet
'The car with its escort rolled across the green sward in front of the old church and came to rest. Von Esslin got out smartly and with springy step made his way into the gloomy interior. He no longer felt timid about the matter – he had convinced himself that he really was acting on behalf of his brother officers. But the church was empty and there were no lights on – only such light as filtered through the tall windows on to the big, undistinguished holy paintings.'

Fort St-André, Villeneuve-lès-Avignon
'Could they be shelling the city? And who? Bang! This time they were awake enough to orient themselves towards the sound; it appeared to come from the densely wooded knoll above Tu Duc where they had once been to hunt for truffles in a holm-oak glade. But who could have got a gun up that steep hill, and for what reason? *Certes*, the whole town of Avignon lay down below it, across the river, with Villeneuve at one side turning the sulky cheeks of her castle towards the left.'

SEBASTIAN

THE ACTION, COVERING THE LAST FEW MONTHS OF THE WAR IN EGYPT AND GENEVA, IS SEEN OBJECTIVELY BUT FROM DIFFERENT ANGLES DEPENDING ON WHICH CHARACTER IS AT ITS CENTRE — AFFAD (SEBASTIAN), CONSTANCE, MNEMIDIS (A PSYCHOPATHIC KILLER) OR SCHWARZ (HEAD OF A SWISS CLINIC). THE CENTRAL CONFRONTATION IS BETWEEN CONSTANCE'S BELIEF IN PSYCHOLOGY (THE EMPIRICISM OF WESTERN SCIENCE) AND AFFAD'S IN GNOSTICISM (THE MYSTICISM OF EASTERN PHILOSOPHY). THEIR LOVE AFFAIR COMPLICATES THE ISSUE AND NEITHER PROVES A WINNER. 'THE DOUBLE CONCERTO' OF BLANFORD'S AND SUTCLIFFE'S NOVELS PLAYS ONLY A MINOR ROLE ALTHOUGH BRUCE, THE NARRATOR OF MONSIEUR, APPEARS AT THE END OF THE BOOK TO DEMAND OF BLANFORD, 'YOUR NOVEL ABOUT THE MATTER IS FINISHED: IT ONLY REMAINS FOR YOU TO SEE IF WE ARE GOING TO LIVE IT ACCORDING TO YOUR FICTION OR ACCORDING TO NEW FACT, NO?' AVIGNON BECKONS ONCE AGAIN.

Coptic monastery at Natrun in the desert
'The monastery gradually rose up out of the sand with its curiously barbaric atmosphere – as if it stood somewhere much more remote, perhaps on the steppes of Middle Asia? The cluster of beehive buildings were glued together in a vast complex of brownish stone: pumice and plaster and whatnot, and the colour of wattle smeared with clay.
This light, friable type of material offered excellent insulation against both desert heat and also the cold of darkness during the winter. The palm groves stood there, silently welcoming, with their weird hieratic forms, benignly awkward.'

STATUE OF LOVERS: AIX

Roast on in ageless loneliness, O Sage
All but abandoned by your fading sex,
With no such drastic animals to keep
At bay, allows his dreams of girls to vex,
Is troubled by young dakinis in his sleep!

In France poor sputtering Sade presides,
And smears the unlucky wench of time,
By tedious repetition dulls
Of all experiences the one sublime—
Phantom caress in sleep the lover culls.

No dissection could as well describe
The science of this woman's head, the beauty
Eaten away by siege, by time, by fire.
Young sorrows incubate in man's desire
Like sonnets engendered by a sleeping rain
Beating on some old poet's hat,
To tell you spring will come again,
The psyche's pious dimorphism means just that.

Wadi-el-Natrun: Monastery of St Pischoi. Paul Hogarth '88

The little lake house, Lake Geneva
'As for Constance, she had at last taken the advice of Schwarz and left for the little lake house which they used for weekends of leave. It lay in a sunken garden and was built over a boat-house containing the precious motor-boat of Schwarz, which he had christened *Freud*.'

Storm on Lake Geneva
'The wind had risen and the waters of the lake were marked with dark prints of paws. The sky had swelled, as ominous as the nervous breakdown she could feel approaching her across the water. She tried once or twice to weep but it did not work; her mind was as dry as a bone. Then it started raining and she ran the last hundred yards to the ferry with her handbag held above her head.'

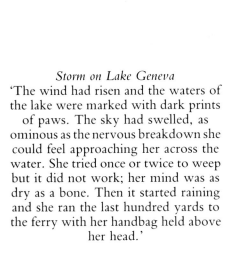

130

Art Nouveau apartment house, Quai Wilson, Geneva
'His mouth set in a grim line. And now here he was in the street he had been seeking, standing before the very house he proposed to visit, utterly sure that everything had been planned for him, so that he might execute an exemplary punishment in the form of a farewell to Swiss medicine. And, by goodness, the door was ajar into the hall, for Constance had slipped out to the nearest pharmacy in search of a febrifuge for her fever-bound lover.'

LAWRENCE DURRELL'S COMMENT:
No particular block in Geneva represents the location of Constance's flat, but the forbidding atmosphere in the painting is entirely appropriate.

Rue Delabre, Geneva old town
'His route took him across the seedier parts of the old town, the poorer quarters, full of *maisons closes* and oriental cafés and moribund hotels; not to speak of the blue cinemas playing pornographic films. The one thing the war had not changed or debased was pornography; if anything far from reducing it, it had caused an efflorescence, an increase. So necessary is it for the scared human ego to belittle a force which it recognizes as being incalculably stronger than itself – the only really uncontrollable force man knows: for even if repressed it bursts out in symbolism, violence, dreaming, madness . . . Mnemidis slackened his pace in order to take in the whole scene with a just pleasure. There were a few sleazy whores already on the street, and the cinemas were rich in promise.'

L D:
The district complements the grotesque disguise as a nun of the lunatic Mnemidis, intent on his murderous visit to Constance's flat.

QUINX

WHEN THE CHARACTERS FROM THE OTHER NOVELS ASSEMBLE AT AVIGNON AFTER THE WAR, THERE IS A SUBSTITUTE TRINITY OF LOVERS — THE TWO 'OGRES' AND BRUCE DREXEL — FOR THAT AT VERFEUILLE IN MONSIEUR AND AT TU DUC IN LIVIA. SUTCLIFFE TAKES THE INITIATIVE AGAINST HIS CREATOR, BLANFORD: 'BUT SURELY WE AREN'T GOING TO LET THE OGRES RE-ENACT THE TERRIBLE HISTORIC MISTAKE WHICH WAS THE THEME OF YOUR GREAT EPOS — THE HEROIC THREESOME OF ROMANCE? COME! IT DIDN'T WORK IN LIFE ANY MORE THAN IT WORKED IN THE NOVEL, ADMIT IT!' IT IS DROPPED, BUT THE TWO DOPPELGANGERS, NOW SEEMINGLY ON EQUAL TERMS, CONTINUE THEIR BIZARRE DOUBLE ACT THROUGH POETIC, PHILOSOPHIC, PROVERBIAL, FANCIFUL AND WITTILY OBSCENE EXCHANGES. DURING THESE DISCOURSES THE PRETENTIOUSLY SERIOUS IS MOCKED. CONSTANCE'S 'FAMILY' HAS BEEN DEVASTATED BY THE WAR — BROTHER, SISTER, HUSBAND, LOVER ALL ARE DEAD — BUT THE 'STATUS QUO ANTE' OF LIVIA IS EFFECTED BY THE REALIZATION OF HER LOVE FOR BLANFORD; THE PUZZLING CONCLUSION OF MONSIEUR MADE MANIFEST. HOWEVER, THE COLOURFUL CONCOURSE OF CHARACTERS GATHERED AT THE END TO WITNESS THE DISCOVERY OF THE TEMPLAR TREASURE AT THE PONT DU GARD IS LEFT SUSPENDED IN TIME. THE FINAL CURTAIN NEVER FALLS. 'THE LOVERS GAVE A SHIVER OF PREMONITION AND BLANFORD THOUGHT THAT IF EVER HE WROTE THE SCENE HE WOULD SAY: "IT WAS AT THIS PRECISE MOMENT THAT REALITY PRIME RUSHED TO THE AID OF FICTION AND THE TOTALLY UNPREDICTABLE BEGAN TO TAKE PLACE!"'

The Camargue
'But the thought of the vanished Sabine touched off other reminiscences of gipsy lore and history with which the nostalgic Sutcliffe enlivened the first part of the journey through the flowering meads of high Provence which soon gave place to the sadder, flatter plains of the Camargue — country of marsh and rivulet and lake where flies and mosquitoes abounded, as well as the sturdy brown bulls of the locality which were raised as cockade fighters for the Provençal bull rings. Here too the characteristic cowboy of the land, the *gardien*, prevailed with his broad-brimmed sombrero and the trident which he sported like a sceptre of office.'

LAWRENCE DURRELL'S COMMENT:
Water plays an important part in the Quintet as it does in Durrell's own life. It creates a sense of vulnerability owing to the danger of flooding. His local river broke its banks again in the winter of '87, and the water lapped at the steps to his front door. The Camargue is less than twenty miles away.

Church of St Sara, Stes-Maries-de-la Mer
'Some of the horse-drawn caravans were brilliantly painted, speaking of Sicily or England. And by the wayside perched their tents in small encampments were the children lay about like litters of cats and puppies in the bluish dust. The tide, however, flowed steadily towards the sea where the little church of the Saint stuck out its abrupt butt towards the beaches, never quite allowing one to forget that it was originally a fort, a defence against the pirates who ravaged this coast.'

133

Paul HOGARTH 87   Avignon St Bénézit Bridge & St Nicolas Chapel

The Pont St-Bénézet, Avignon 'Running along the grey-green river they had seen the famous broken bridge, still pointing its reproachful finger across the water towards the waterless *garrigue*. Neither Blanford nor Sutcliffe could resist the prompting to hum out:
Sur le pont d'Avignon · on y pense, on y pense . . . sur le pont d'Avignon · on y pense, tout en rond!
"How much longer have we got together?" asked Blanford and his alter ego replied: "One more book, one more river. Then body and soul must end their association. I know. It's too short. It's the only criticism one can make of life. It's too short to learn anything."'

135

The Artist's Journal

I arrive in Avignon and follow the example of both Henry James and Lawrence Durrell by establishing myself at the Hôtel d'Europe in the Place Crillon. The former sixteenth-century palace is a haven of peace; coolly elegant within a shady courtyard. The stone sundial is in place above the entrance door as is the moss-encrusted fountain under the old plane tree.

After an exploratory walkabout in the Balance quarter I discover much has changed since my last visit in the Sixties. Not, as in Alexandria, demolished but restored and sanitized as a living museum for tourists. Indeed, some of the more celebrated sights have been so well preserved, they look almost new. I walk down to the Ramparts and depict the ruined Pont St-Bénézet with its fort-like chapel of St Nicholas. Across the river lies the melancholy Tower of Philippe-le-Bel who brought the Popes to Avignon in the first place. The Place du Palais, dominated by the cliff-like façade of the Palace of the Popes resembles a stage set for a motley company of strolling musicians, pavement artists and pedlars of cheap jewellery. All regard me with suspicion as the tourists begin to appear. A hairy black-maned group of Peruvian Indians begin to play the skirling airs of the Andes. But as they go through one number after another, I recall the late Brendan Behan's quip about the folk music of his native land, 'Bejasus', he rasped, 'when you've heard one, you've heard the bloody lot!'

I have a pleasant Sunday lunch with Lawrence Durrell at the Maison du Quatre Vents, a little restaurant just outside the front gates of the Château Villevieille. Strangely enough – although not, of course, in the Alpilles – this turns out to be the original of his 'Château Verfeuille' the country house of the young French diplomat, Piers de Nogaret, and one of the more important settings in *Monsieur*. We chat about architecture and I observe that it plays an important part in his writing, 'It's the vital outer skin,' he replies.

I find this to be especially true some weeks later in Venice, another setting for *Monsieur*. Like the obsessed novelist, Robin Sutcliffe, I wander about the shadowy purlieus of the Grand Canal, searching for a vantage point from where I might depict 'the orchestra of divine buildings' as Durrell described Venice, 'over water-wobbled, gondola-scratched canals'. People peep over my shoulders even before I make a single pencil stroke. The pressures of curiosity are enormous in a city which is, after all, a living theatre in which both citizen and tourist feel impelled to participate.

I find a spot on the Ponte dell'Accademia, the first point from which one can view the Grand Canal in all its ascending majesty. On the immediate left is the seventeenth-century palace Ca' Barbaro. During the nineteenth century, it was owned by the wealthy Daniel Curtis family of Boston and became the haunt of celebrated artists and writers. Monet and Sargent were their guests and had studios there: as was Henry James who placed part of

The Wings of the Dove in the palace. On the right are the palaces Contarini dal Zaffo, Ca' Balbi-Valier and Ca' Loredan. In the distance is the Dogana di Mare or Customs House with its twin Atlases holding up the golden ball with the weathervane of Fortune on top. The Salute dominates the skyline and, god forbid, television antennae. I think of Canaletto and use shadows to sharpen the effect of my extended design.

Midway through my musings, a fanfare of trumpets heralds a stately convoy of ornate barges propelled by stalwart gondoliers in equally splendid garb. One huge barge, or *comacina*, with a crimson banner trailing astern, leads the others in solemn procession. By chance, I am witness to the historical regatta celebrating the Festival of the Ascension and the marriage of the city with the sea: a spectacle from the bygone era of the Venetian Republic which even the unhappy Sutcliffe would have welcomed as a momentary diversion from the defection of his beloved Pia.

LIVIA

The Château of Tu Duc, inherited by Constance from a maiden aunt, provides a nostalgic focus for the *dramatis personae* of THE AVIGNON QUINTET; a second home for some and a point of no return for others. Yet it is one of Durrell's few fictitious settings 'culled' as he told me, 'from the stockpot'. Tu Duc, it transpires, is a country estate, a Provençal *mas* or large manor farm. Since our meeting in Sommières I have been looking for a possible candidate but so far without success. Then just off the D750 Tarascon-Arles road I suddenly spot a big old place amidst a small wood of plane trees. I drive up a quiet lane to find a sadly abandoned Romanesque manor complete with *pigeonnier* on its outer perimeter, walls draped with mattresses of ivy and vine. Mas Mottet, like Tu Duc itself it is in a state of disrepair, gutters are twisted and full of leaves. I'm intrigued by the romantic atmosphere which pervades the old *mas*. And with no one around to disturb me, I unfold my stool and draw for much of the afternoon.

Spending a day in the Clothdyers' Quarter in Avignon, I look for the little Chapel of the Grey Penitents in the Rue des Teinturiers. The Chapel is mentioned as a port-of-call for Felix Chatto's walkabout in *Livia* and is also the scene in *Constance* of von Esslin's search for a German-speaking priest to hear his confession.

The tranquil waters of the canal with the old water-wheels of the clothdyers follow a winding tree-lined cobbled street more reminiscent of Flemish Bruges than Provençal Avignon.

The marvellously comic sequence wherein Prince Hassad accompanied by his dogs, is taken by the ubiquitous Quatrefages to Riquiqui's brothel in an unnamed street behind the Hôtel de Ville prompts me to hope that I may find an image to match. But I draw a complete blank.

Low life has long vanished from the Old Town. The medieval streets of the Balance Quarter are no longer inhabited by prostitutes and gypsies. The bars and brothels of yesteryear are now boutiques, tourist gift-shops and fashionable restaurants.

Blanford's nostalgic recollection of a visit to the Fontaine-de-Vaucluse seems reason enough to pay a visit to the resurgent stream, the source of the River Sorgues. The little town bustles with weekend visitors who climb the path to the spring. Translucent green waters rush below a vast cliff lined with the fragmented ruins of an ancient castle. But most visitors appear unmoved by the spectacle. Petrarch and his lady Laura have for long been the rival attraction. But can this be the reason for the scores of young couples who stroll about as if in a trance?

To the east of Avignon lies the Pont du Gard, that majestic Roman aqueduct which has been a place of pilgrimage ever since the Grand Tour. I decide not to add my name to that illustrious band of artist-travellers who have depicted the famous edifice. Instead, I choose the setting of Prince Hassad's spree, the rambling old-fashioned and somewhat eccentric Auberge des Aubergines with its chalet-esque façade enlivened by balconies of concrete antlers so beloved by the builders of the *fin-de-siècle*.

CONSTANCE

More Avignon settings are discovered, among them, the Musée Calvet in the Préfecture Quarter. It was here that Blanford peeped into the courtyard to suffer another poignant pang, a memory of Livia standing there reciting a line from Goethe. Later, I cross the Rhône to Villeneuve-lès-Avignon to view the massive fortress of St André and depict the grim old gate-towers which flank the entrance to the ruins of a vast thirteenth-century Benedictine monastery and what was once the village of St André. I draw the Hôtel d'Europe which now looks anything but 'hopelessly unkempt'. Its genial manager is fascinated to learn of the part played by the Hôtel in *Constance*, whose heroine stayed there on her return visit to Avignon as a representative of the Red Cross.

Another setting, Montfavet, wasn't quite as I'd expected it to be. The little old church, the scene of von Esslin's confession, turns out to be impressively large as it was once a part of a fourteenth-century monastery. The green sward is now a car park jammed with the vehicles of farmers and townspeople.

In Geneva I am delighted to find that the Bar de la Navigation still exists at the the corner of the Rue du Môle and the Place de la Navigation. Strangely enough, or perhaps it's my imagination, the old bar, now the Café de la Navigation, still retains the ambience of a local rendezvous used by intelligence operatives. It is far from being sophisticated, with its somewhat raffish company of workingmen (active and retired), battered old prostitutes and piratical sailors who crew the steamboats on nearby Lake Geneva.

I return to the Egyptian pages of my journal to note further settings for *Constance*. These include the remarkable Palace of Montaza on the eastern fringes of Alexandria and the Monastery of Aby Fahym. The Palace of Montaza, which Durrell describes as his first experience of Egyptian Baroque, is one of the most eccentric buildings I have seen, let alone drawn. Like Durrell, I fall in love with the place. I certainly need to as it takes me three hours to draw it. Originally built by Khedive Abbas II, it was restored by King Fuad I to please, it is said, his Austrian mistress. The main building is built in Turkish Beaux-Arts style with hundreds of large spiky iron lamps and an enormous central tower based on that of the Palazzo Vecchio in Florence. During World War I, the palace became a military hospital. E. M. Forster, stationed in Alexandria as a Red Cross orderly, convalesced there from a bout of hepatitis.

I have to have a bird's-eye view to bring out its megalomaniacal character to the full. Moreover, showers between sunshine made it necessary to work undercover. A sixth-floor hotel balcony overlooking the palace would be an ideal vantage point. Luckily, one was at hand at the nearby Palestine Hotel. Obligingly, the management is persuaded to place one at my disposal for the day.

On the other hand, the Monastery of Aby Fahym, the scene of the tragic accidental death of Sam, turns out to be 'out of the stockpot'. But on a visit to the Coptic monasteries of Wadi-al-Natrun, I unexpectedly find a substitute in the ancient Keep or *Kasr* and bell-tower of the Church of the Elders at Deir Makaryus, complete with a 'Bridge of Sighs'.

SEBASTIAN

The exacting task of tracking down the places described by Durrell, and then reflecting how best to depict them, never fails to fascinate me. Moreover, it is a task which differs from one country to another, and from one city to another. Geneva, for example, in possessing the overtones of the Mediterranean and Central Europe, unexpectedly offers a range of unusual subjects. Notably, Lake Geneva, which plays a major role in *Sebastian*, contributes several settings. Besides the long elegantly funnelled Victorian steamboats alongside the Quai de Mont-Blanc, is Schwarz's little lake house where he kept the motorboat, *Freud*. On the Quai Wilson is the apartment house where Constance lived, the scene of Affad's murder by the pyschopath Mnemidis.

Elsewhere I discover the 'Old Bavaria' on the Boulevard St Georges. Alas, all that remains of the Austro-Hungarian furnishings is a crudely painted window sign of a moustached Bavarian in folk costume quaffing a huge stein of lager. The bar is now known as the Bar Apollo. An acquaintance, the English-speaking newsagent opposite the Bar de la Navigation, tells me that the Old Geneva of blue movies and the *maison close* which Larry placed in the Rue Delabre, has long since gone. What little remains, he adds, is in the Rue de la Cité, a precipitous stairway of a street in the Vieille Ville, or Old Town. I hope the city fathers will forgive me for enlivening my night-scene in that street with a blue movie poster culled from a much more venal street in Zurich's Old Town quarter.

Egypt provides an unusual location at Wadi-al-Natrun or Valley of Soda. Some 50 kilometres south-west of Alexandria the Valley has for the past seventeen centuries been a Christian enclave in this staunchly Moslem land. Despite the gradual encroachment of civilization in the shape of nearby Sadat City and the Desert Motorway, the four great Coptic monasteries are still here. One of them, Deir-al-Anba Bishay, or Monastery of St Pischoi is the scene of Affad's last visit to his estranged wife, Lily, who has retreated to the ancient monastery to live alone in an isolated cell.

As I drive through groves of palm and olive, the monastery rises out of the desert before my eyes, metamorphosing like a mirage from the steppes of Central Asia. Even to come here by car instead of by camel seems a heretical act. Like Affad, I lift the heavy iron knocker and bang it down on the studded wooden door. A heavily-bearded monk opens up and bids me enter an ancient courtyard where black-robed monks glide about. I am introduced to their principal, Father Shedrak, an ardent proselytizer. Over a glass of tea, he talks about the influence of the Copts. St Patrick was a disciple of a Coptic monk, as were St Boniface of Munich and St Maurice (after whom St Moritz was named). The good father courteously grants me permission to draw the monastery and asks workmen repairing the ninth-century Church of St Bishay to lend me a primitive ladder. Although the rungs are almost a half-metre apart, this enables me to depict the incredible beehive-domed older buildings of the monastery from a nearby rooftop: a hair-raising exercise on an old roof of friable, plaster-like material littered with what looks like the detritus of centuries.

QUINX

Anyone who has seen the Pont St-Bénézet, Avignon's famous ruined bridge, silhouetted against the dying light of a summer evening is not likely to forget the spectacle. Blanford and Sutcliffe were so affected that they hummed out the nursery rhyme. Completed by 1190, the bridge took twelve years to build but only four arches of the original twenty-two remain. Henry James thought it didn't matter, 'for (the arches) stop', he wrote, 'in such a sketchable manner in mid-stream'. He is quite right.

A few days later, I leave Avignon to enter the strange and somewhat desolate delta of the Petit Camargue. Here and there I pass an *ousteau* or small farm with its *bergerie* or sheepbarn, surrounded by reclaimed, desalinated pastures which sustain huge herds of sheep. Red-tipped bands of ochre-stemmed bullrushes mark off vast salt marshlands which stretch to infinity on both sides of the straight D570, the haunt of the black long-horned Camargue bull and attendant herds of half-wild cattle. The little fishing town of Stes-Maries-de-la-Mer comes into view, a place of legendary origin and the celebrated venue of a popular gypsy pilgrimage every May. Indeed, the St Sara Festival provides another setting for *Quinx*, but sadly I have missed the event. An imposing fortified church, the Church of St Sara rises above the town and adjacent marshlands like an ancient Greek *pharos* or lighthouse. In and around the town are little old ladies, some of whom sit in the doorways of their houses showing off the traditional black and white folk costume. Fishing boats, rather different to those painted by Van Gogh a century ago, tie up in the quay-side to disgorge their catches of bass and monkfish, eel and zander.

Stes-Maries-de-la-Mer faces the Mediterranean on the south side and the Étang des Launes on the west. The *étang* or inlet resembles a nature reserve, an idyllic scene of marsh and water enlivened by flocks of wildfowl, egrets, flamingos and ibises: all of which make a strong emotional appeal to the landscape painter in me. And when I consult my notes and find it is also a setting for *Quinx*, there's no holding me back. To draw or paint a landscape, however, one has to have peace and quiet. But unexpectedly, I find the conditions are almost perfect. Other than a mere handful of latter-day German *Wandervögel* fast asleep within their mobile homes, and the odd post-hippy backpacker, there are for once, few tourists about. I can therefore relax to analyse and depict the lyrical qualities of the scene before me. I devise a composition in Japanese fashion with a high horizon line before I move on to add various focal points such as a *cabane* (the two-roomed farmhouse of the mounted cowboy-like *gardiens*) with its rush-thatched roof and white walls which curve into an apse at the north end, tipped by a wooden crucifix sloped against the prevailing mistral. I add the occasional accent of a flat-bottomed fishing boat, clumps of trees, flocks of wild fowl and the odd flamingo or egret. And finally, a *gardien* himself with his wide-brimmed hat, who obligingly rides by on his white *losir* or Arab breed of horse.

On leaving Provence, Larry informs me that he has bought a burial plot in the cemetery of St Julien de Montredon, Salinelles, 'Francis Kyle' I tell him 'doesn't like me drawing graveyards and cemeteries.' 'That's between you and your maker.' Larry replies with a chuckle.

THE GREEK ISLANDS CORFU

OF SOME 2,000 ISLANDS, NOT ALL INHABITED, 56 OF THE MORE INTERESTING AND ACCESSIBLE ARE VISITED. THE VARIETY IS IMPRESSIVE, RANGING FROM THE ROMANTIC AND LUXURIANT IONIAN GROUP TO THE 'PURE, VERTICAL, DRAMATIC' AEGEAN; FROM LARGE ISLANDS CRAMMED WITH HISTORY LIKE CRETE TO LITTLE PARADISES LIKE IOS. THE ACCOUNT IS NOT SPARING IN PRAISE — 'IT IS LIKE INHABITING A RAINBOW' (MYKONOS) — OR DENIGRATION — 'A DAMNABLY DULL ISLAND' (LEMNOS). PERSONAL IMPRESSIONS AND ANECDOTES ARE MINGLED WITH HISTORICAL AND PHILOSOPHICAL OBSERVATIONS. GREEK HOSPITALITY REACHES ITS APOGEE IN CRETE: 'AND EVEN TODAY IT IS DANGEROUS TO EXPRESS ADMIRATION FOR SOMETHING, FOR YOU WILL CERTAINLY FIND IT IN YOUR BAGGAGE AS A FAREWELL GIFT WHEN YOU LEAVE. YOU CANNOT REFUSE. THEY ARE ADAMANT. I KNEW A LADY WHO GOT A BABY THIS WAY.' THE PAGAN PAST AND THE CHRISTIAN PRESENT ARE INDIVISIBLE; ODYSSEUS OF ITHACA AND APHRODITE OF CYTHERA ARE AS MUCH A PRESENCE AS ST SPIRIDION OF CORFU OR THE VIRGIN OF TINOS. THE FINAL FUSION IS SEEN WHEN DIONYSUS APPEARS AS BOTH PAGAN GOD AND CHRISTIAN SAINT. LEGEND AND HISTORY OVERLAP. IDIOSYN-CRATIC TIPS FOR TOURISTS — BINOCULARS INSTEAD OF CAMERAS AND FREUD'S TOTEM AND TABOO FOR HOLIDAY READING — JOSTLE MORE SERIOUS INSIGHTS: 'ALL HABITS, OF COURSE, STEM FROM CLIMATE WHICH, IN A SUBTLE, UNOBTRUSIVE MANNER, DICTATES EVERYTHING ABOUT THE WAY WE LIVE, AND OFTEN ABOUT THE WAY WE LOVE.'

Lesseps Arcade
'The old town is set down gracefully upon the wide tree-lined esplanade, whose arcades are of French provenance and were intended (they do) to echo the Rue de Rivoli. The best cafés are here and the friendliest waiters in all Christendom.'

140

Monastery of Paleocastrizza
'There are astonishingly few harbours on the other side of the island – indeed only one really meriting the name. That is at the famous Paleocastrizza, now half ruined by the tourist promoter, though the old monastery on its hillock is still a dream-place and the magnificent cliffs upon which Lakones stands offer stupendous views worthy of Taormina.'

LAWRENCE DURRELL'S COMMENT:
What made it so felicitous is its setting with the thunder of the sea and the strength of the wind.

141

CRETE

Venetian Arsenals, Chanea

L D:
Because the island is so large, almost a subcontinent, it has been the centre of military and naval activity, hence the arsenals.

142

MYKONOS

Lawrence Durrell's comment: Two summers were spent there when the only other visitor was George Seferis, an ambassador on shore-leave. For many years it was the summer home of Yehudi and Diana Menuhin, old friends, until over-population drove them away. Durrell first met Diana in Cairo when she was dancing in *The Merry Widow* for ENSA during the War. The poem 'Mareotis' is dedicated to her and she used it as an introduction to her autobiography.

Street in the Kastro Quarter
'Here plane geometry takes wing and becomes curved of surface. The little square boxes of houses are pure, unplanned expressions of the islanders' inner metric. Everywhere the tiny chapels bud and proliferate like some crazy illustration of genetic fission; self-multiplying breasts, fused one upon the other, joined like the separate cloves which go to make a garlic-head or an orange; compartmented upon the same mathematical principle as the pomegranate-fruit which nods its toy crown at you over many a walled garden gate.'

L D:
Particularly memorable are the tavernas where fish was deeper fried than anywhere else and the wine stronger than in most islands.

LIMITS: MYKONOS WINDMILLS

The pure form, then, must be the blue silence
And the archaic shape of whiteness posed
On blueness utterly bemused, a sort of coyness
Which garners the wind of the four quarters.
I would tear out a leaf and spread it,
The second skin of music after dark,
Then with a drypoint etch in
Everything that won't talk back like frost
Perhaps some profitable look or fused embrace
Bury it here full of its gay informal logic
Like a rose upon a coffin full
Of foreknowledge of the breathing game,
The bent bow of your love aimed at the sky . .

How loud the perfume of common gin,
How morose the pigment that covers a lipid,
How soft the equal gauze of quits,
How purple the pits of amazing berries.
And all the time death quietly sits and knits:
Your sake, my sake, his sake, her sake,

Everyone is entitled to just one sake.

House in the Venetian Quarter
'Its colonnades and curling streets,
with their kennel-like houses,
sprouting extravagant balconies of
tottering painted wood, lead on and
on, turning slowly inward upon
themselves to form labyrinths, hazing–
in all sense of direction until one
surrenders to the knowledge that one is
irremediably lost in a village hardly
bigger than Hampstead.'

Windmills
'You will have the queerest feeling of
sadness as your boat levels off and
begins to cross the two or three sea
miles which separate it from Mykonos
– where all is shining calm and silence,
and where the quiet windmills with
their grey sails turn all the time; for
never for a second does the wind
let up.'

Paraportiani Church
'As for the three hundred and forty
little Orthodox chapels in the capital,
they all seem to be private property,
belonging to the various families who,
at one time or another, had estates in
the island. They are all tiny, and
seemingly decorated *con furioso* by
unbalanced monks with Sicilian
backgrounds.'

L D:
The island gives the impression of such
brilliant whiteness that it might almost
be under snow.

145

PAROS

The Venetian Castle
'The standard Venetian castle rides the
traditional acropolis crown of the
ancient city. The ancient stone has been
run into the old walls in a most flagrant
way, and here and there you will find
rows of drums and columns seized
from a now vanished temple to Hera.
So one age wolfs the glories of its
predecessor.'

The Mavrogeni Fountain, Paroika
'What is the secret of its charm – the feeling of zestful ease it gives you while you navigate those dazzling white streets punctuated with whole balconies and bowers of flowers in bloom? The two long, main streets are more or less parallel, and they have been criss-crossed and stitched with interconnecting lanes of pure whiteness, which give the impression of being simply felicitous afterthoughts.'

RHODES

Lindos 'The little town below, with its intricate cobbled streets and blazing
whitewashed walls, lies very still. There seem to be few taverns, few open
spaces under a plane tree where one can put a table and a chair.
The main *taverna*, however, is beautifully situated just outside the citadel
entrance under a tree, and others have sprung up in recent years.
You can rent rooms in the town of Lindos, which drowses its life away,
hardly troubled by the coming and going of the big buses with their sightseers.'

SKIATHOS

St Nicholas Church and Clock Tower

'Here water and cypresses and shade give one back a sense of plenitude and peace – particularly on Skiathos, the beauty of the group,
whose perched capital neatly divides a harbour like a *mons veneris*; its dazzling white houses built as if from lump sugar, its labyrinth of quizzical churches.'

149

SAMOS

THE SIRENS

Trembling they appear, the Siren isles,
Bequeathing lavender and molten rose,

Reflecting in the white caves of our sails
Melodious capes of fancy and of terror,

Where now the singers surface at the prow,
Begin the famous, pitiless, wounded singing . . .

Ulysses watching, like many a hero since,
Thinks: 'Voyages and privations!

The loutish sea which swallows up our loves,
Lying windless under a sky of lilac,

Far from our home, the longed-for landfall . . .
By God! They choose their time, the Sirens.'

Every poet and hero has to face them,
The glittering temptresses of his distraction,

The penalties which seek him for a hostage.
Homer and Milton: both were punished in their gift.

Landscape near Vathi

The Temple of Hera
'The third was the temple of Hera which was one of the wonders of the ancient world, and of which little now remains except the site, starkly beautiful on its headland where goats browse and untiring eagles weave overhead. Cape Colonna, as the place is called, has priceless views of the mainland from every spur; but of Hera's temple only a single column marked the spot when last I was there.'

Monastery of Zoodóhos Pigí

Fortress of Logothetis and Church of the Transfiguration

Caldera and islets Palea and Nea Kameni
'And once you sail into the huge bowl which the Santorin explosion created – eighteen miles round the inner rim – you find yourself confronted with something quite unlike the rest of the Cyclades. The smell of sulphur and the pit still seems to hang in the air, giving a diabolical flavour to the scenery which, without too much imagination, could conjure up a back drop suitable for a stage hell.'

152

Santorini: Caldera & the Islets
Palea & Nea Kameni

SANTORIN

153

The Artist's Journal

I enter the white-washed labyrinthine streets of Mykonos Old Town feeling like Alice in Wonderland. Cube-like houses cling together like beehives on different levels with arches and overhanging balconies. Churches and chapels abound, some 340 in number. Throughout the centuries, sailors in danger pledged themselves to build one if they were saved by what they believed to be the Almighty. Even more distinctive because of their location are the windmills, which ground the grain to produce the flour for the bakeries which traditionally supplied the fleets of the Byzantines, Venetians, Turks, French, Russians and British with vast quantities of bread. Only five remain, symbols of the tenacious ingenuity of the fishermen and farmers that sought to consolidate their existence on this spare and rocky island.

Our diminutive Fokker aircraft with its eighteen passengers alights like a fly on the landing strip of Paros. Soon the bus enters Paroika, a crumbly tourist boomtown built around a pleasant old quarter. Opposite my hotel is a memento of the 1821 Revolution, the white marble Mavrogeni Fountain named after Manto Mavrogenius, a heroine of that struggle against the Turks. Throughout the classical period, Paros prospered from quarrying and exporting its flawless white marble, much prized by architects and sculptors. To the north, Naousa yields a scene of its famous harbour which at various times played a vital part in the island's checkered history. A Byzantine settlement flourished here followed by the Venetians who built the fortress whose ruins can be seen in my picture. Today, the ancient harbour is the home port of a large fishing fleet kept busy by the insatiable appetites of the tourist hordes.

Santorin is easily the most spectacular island of them all, an awe-inspiring configuration or rock, sea and sky. Durrell's description, that it possesses a diabolical flavour, like a backdrop for a stage hell, is especially apt. I am a guest of an Athenian friend, whose summer house has a dramatic dress-circle view of the sea-filled crater set in the Bay of Anthios with Fira or Thera clinging to a precipitous ridge overlooking a vast roadstead of 'wine-dark' sea.

In Fira itself, scenes reminiscent of holidays abroad in the Victorian era take place. Fiercely moustached muleteers ambush chosen victims with vociferous cries. The hapless tourists who succumb condemn themselves to riding muleback up a vertiginous stairway of 587 steps in the broiling heat.

I find Oia, or Ia, even more phantasmagoric. Venetian-style villas and boxy snow-white houses line narrow lanes which encircle the crest of a mountain of multi-coloured volcanic strata, like the icing on an awesomely elaborate wedding cake for giants.

I am busily drawing my first Greek monastery on Corfu, at Paleocastrizza. Its tranquil precincts are redolent with crimson bougainvillaea which flourish luxuriantly against walls of white and yellow. But no sooner have I

The house of the writer Alexandros Padiamantis

got started than I am disturbed by a band of giggling tourists who descend about me to drop coins down the courtyard well and beer-cans on the flower-beds.

The French who briefly occupied Corfu took a great interest in the appearance of the Old Town. One of its most striking buildings, the Liston, occupies half of its western side of the Spianada or *platia*, an arcaded terrace designed in the French Empire style by Mathieu de Lesseps, father of Ferdinand, the builder of the Suez Canal, and inspired by the Rue de Rivoli in Paris.

From the air, most Greek islands look like the backs of oyster shells. Occasionally, they are enlivened by verdant patches of cypress and pine, and fishing villages of red-roofed dazzlingly white houses. In the summer, Skiathos is all these things. But now it is late October and a spell of turbulent weather has reduced the island's colour to a greyness reminiscent of an island off the west coast of Scotland.

I am fortunate indeed, to discover that Skiathos was home for two distinguished Greek writers, Alexandros Moraitidou (1850–1929) and Alexandros Padiamantis (1851–1911) whose picturesque houses provide good subjects for my restless pencil. I am even more fortunate on the morning of my last day. The weather clears up sufficiently for me to climb to a vantage point above the town. From here I depict the Church of St Nicholas and its Clock Tower against a dramatic vista of sea and sky.

Samos, a green and hilly island, faces Turkey across a narrow strait but two kilometres away. Samos Town is the port district of the capital, Vathi. The old quarter, rises in the hills above, a world in itself with old Byzantine chapels and vineyards. Turkish-style wooden houses with overhanging upper floors line precipitous streets, inhabited by fairy-tale characters who wash doorsteps, ask me how old I am, or clutch plastic bags of fresh sardines. *Bouzouki* from a nearby café provides pleasant background music as I draw.

Elsewhere, I depict the Fortress of Logothetis at Pithagorion and the Temple Shrine of Hera. Another vertiginous journey takes me to the Monastery of Zoodóhos Pigí, perched on a windswept mountain facing Turkey over the Samos Strait. I take cover from the ferocious north wind behind juniper bushes, hardly daring to glance at the precipitous cliffs and raging sea below.

As in 1876, when Edward Lear visited Crete, Old Chanea clusters around the harbour. And although there is the odd monument from the days of the Turkish occupation, the town still remains essentially Venetian in character. Along the southern edge of the *Limani* or inner harbour, Venetian *arsenali*, or domed dockyards, still stand, unexpectedly evocative examples of early Renaissance marine architecture.

Lear journeyed on mountain trails to the Monastery of Arkádhi on horseback. Over a century later, it is hardly a less arduous journey by car along narrow twisting mountain roads to reach its impressive site on the edge of a vast plateau overlooking a wild and craggy gorge. Two years after Lear's visit, the Monastery was refuge for some 1,000 Cretan patriots who after holding out against 12,000 Turkish soldiers, decided to blow themselves up in their powder magazine rather than surrender. Lear's host, Gabriel Marinákis, the Abbot, and a resistance leader, died with over 800 freedom fighters and their women and children.

Rhodes Town with its Gothic heritage, its mosques and its Art Deco, has cast such a spell, that I am reluctant to leave, but I do need to see more of this blessed isle and as I recall the passion of Larry's enthusiasm for Lindos in his *Greek Islands*, I make the effort and drive there. After an hour or so, a sleepy valley comes into view. Then suddenly, a dramatic and breathtaking spectacle presents itself. Against a turquoise sea, massive ramparts are crowned with the ruins of a classical temple and a medieval fortress. Below, intricate stairways of streets are lined with whitewashed houses. All combine to make Lindos a quintessential image of the Mediterranean Shore, on which a quartet of life-styles—from classical antiquity through Romanesque and Gothic to Islam—have left their mark.

LAWRENCE DURRELL: A SELECT BIBLIOGRAPHY

(Extracts from the following are reproduced by kind permission of Faber and Faber Ltd)

NOVELS

The Black Book Copyright 1938 by Lawrence Durrell, © Lawrence Durrell 1959;
The Dark Labyrinth © Lawrence Durrell 1958 (originally published as *Cefalû* Copyright 1947 by Lawrence Durrell)

THE ALEXANDRIA QUARTET

Justine Copyright © 1957 by Lawrence Durrell; *Balthazar* Copyright © 1958 by Lawrence Durrell;
Mountolive Copyright © 1958 by Lawrence Durrell; *Clea* Copyright © 1960 by Lawrence Durrell

THE REVOLT OF APHRODITE

Tunc © Lawrence Durrell 1968; *Nunquam* © Lawrence Durrell 1970

THE AVIGNON QUINTET

Monsieur © Lawrence Durrell 1974; *Livia* © Lawrence Durrell 1978;
Constance © Lawrence Durrell 1979, 1982; *Sebastian* © Lawrence Durrell 1983; *Quinx* © Lawrence Durrell 1985

TRAVEL

Prospero's Cell Copyright 1945 by Lawrence Durrell; *Reflections on a Marine Venus* Copyright 1953 by Lawrence Durrell;
Bitter Lemons © Lawrence Durrell 1957; *Sicilian Carousel* © Lawrence Durrell 1977; *The Greek Islands* © Lawrence Durrell 1978
reproduced by permission of the Rainbird Publishing Group Ltd

POETRY

Collected Poems © Lawrence Durrell 1957, 1960, 1968, 1974, 1977, 1980 and 1985

LETTERS AND ESSAYS

Spirit of Place (Edited by Alan G. Thomas) © Lawrence Durrell 1969

FOR YOUNG PEOPLE

White Eagles over Serbia © Lawrence Durrell 1957

USA

Extracts from *The Dark Labyrinth, Bitter Lemons, Justine, Balthazar, Clea* and *Mountolive* are reproduced by permission of the publishers
E. P. Dutton, a division of NAL Penguin Inc.

Extracts from *The Revolt of Aphrodite, Quinx, Sicilian Carousel* and *Collected Poems* are reproduced by permission of the publishers Viking Penguin Inc.

ALSO BY PAUL HOGARTH

GAZETTEER

THE PLEIADES

The Pleiades are sinking calm as paint,
And earth's huge camber follows out,
Turning in sleep, the oceanic curve,

Defined in concave like a human eye
Or cheek pressed warm on the dark's cheek,
Like dancers to a music they deserve.

This balcony, a moon-anointed shelf
Above a silent garden holds my bed.
I slept. But the dispiriting autumn moon,

In her slow expurgation of the sky
Needs company: is brooding on the dead,
And so am I now, so am I.

The Chapel of St Julien de Mondtredon, Salinelles

A
Sketch Map
of where the
drawings & Watercolours
were made

SPAIN

FRANCE

●Zuric
SWITZERLAN
●Gene
Rhone
PROVENCE
●Avign
CE

Saintes-Marie
de-la-Mer

MEDITERR